★ **It's My State!** ★ ★ ★ ★ ★ ★

MICHIGAN

The Great Lakes State

Johannah Haney, Richard Hantula, and Petra Miller

Cavendish
Square

New York

Published in 2017 by Cavendish Square Publishing, LLC
243 5th Avenue, Suite 136, New York, NY 10016

Third Edition

Website: cavendishsq.com

This publication represents the opinions and views of the author based on his or her personal experience, knowledge, and research. The information in this book serves as a general guide only. The author and publisher have used their best efforts in preparing this book and disclaim liability rising directly or indirectly from the use and application of this book.

CPSIA Compliance Information: Batch #CS16CSQ

All websites were available and accurate when this book was sent to press.

Library of Congress Cataloging-in-Publication Data
Names: Haney, Johannah, author. | Hantula, Richard, author. | Miller, Petra, author.
Title: Michigan / Johannah Haney, Richard Hantula, and Petra Miller.
Description: New York : Cavendish Square Publishing, 2017. | Series: It's my state! | Includes index. | Description based on print version record and CIP data provided by publisher; resource not viewed.
Identifiers: LCCN 2015046000 (print) | LCCN 2015043529 (ebook) | ISBN 9781627131650 (ebook) | ISBN 9781627131636 (library bound)
Subjects: LCSH: Michigan--Juvenile literature.
Classification: LCC F566.3 (print) | LCC F566.3 .H36 2017 (ebook) | DDC 977.4—dc23
LC record available at http://lccn.loc.gov/2015046000

Editorial Director: David McNamara
Editor: Fletcher Doyle
Copy Editor: Nathan Heidelberger
Art Director: Jeffrey Talbot
Designer: Alan Sliwinski
Production Assistant: Karol Szymczuk
Photo Research: J8 Media

The photographs in this book are used by permission and through the courtesy of: SNEHIT/Shutterstock.com, cover; Vaclav Volrab/Shutterstock.com, 4; John Glover/Alamy, 4; David Stuckel/Alamy, 4; Jeff Feverston/Shutterstock.com, 5; Jim Dufresne/Associated Press, 5; Ross Frid/Alamy, 5; Kenneth Keifer/Shutterstock. com, 6; Spring Images/Alamy, 8; Isle Royale on Page 10 - Jim West/Alamy, 9; Westgraphix LLC, 10; Peter Arnold, Inc./Alamy, 12; Daniel Dempster Photography/ Alamy, 13; mofotodesigns/iStock/Thinkstock, 14; Kremerbi/File:Gilmore Car Museum, Hickory Corners, Michigan USA - 1934 Auburns.JPG/Wikimedia Commons, 14; ehrlif/Shutterstock.com, 14; AP Photo/Mark Bialek, 15; Susan Montgomery/Shutterstock.com, 15; Doxieone Photography/Moment Open/Getty Images, 15; Peter Arnold, Inc./Alamy, 16; Corbis Flirt/Alamy, 17; Joel Trick of U.S. Fish and Wildlife Service Headquarters/File:Dendroica kirtlandii -Michigan, USA -male-8 (4).jpg/ Wikimedia Commons, 19; Jennifer Brown/Alamy, 20; Steffen Hauser/botanikfoto/Alamy, 20; Buddy Mays/Alamy, 20; Mark Bridger/Shutterstock.com, 21; Trofimov Pavel/Shutterstock.com, 21; Steve Oehlenschlager/Shutterstock.com, 21; AP Photo/Michigan State Archives, 22; Milwaukee Public Museum, 24; North Wind Picture Archives/Alamy, 25; © iStockphoto.com/akaplummer, 27; North Wind Picture Archives/Alamy, 29; Everett Historical/Shutterstock.com, 32; Superstock/Superstock, 33; Eyecon Images/Alamy, 34; Chris Raboir Sports Photography/Alamy, 35; Getty Images News/Getty Images, 35; Phil Vettel/Chicago Tribune/MCT via Getty Images, 34; Archive Photos/Getty Images, 37; Stanislaw Tokarski/Shutterstock.com, 38; Archive Photos/Getty Images, 40; Bloomberg/Getty Images, 41; Susan Montgomery/ Shutterstock.com, 44; Wolfgang Kaehler/Superstock, 46; doma/Shutterstock.com, 47; Earl Gibson III/WireImage/Getty Images, 48; Debby Wong/Shutterstock.com, 48; Archive Photos/Getty Images, 48; Getty Images Entertainment/Getty Images, 49; Ga Fullner/Shutterstock.com, 49; Imagebroker.net/Superstock, 49; Steve Liss/ The LIFE Images Collection/Getty Images, 51; Dennis MacDonald/Alamy, 53; AP Photo/The Grand Rapids Press, Cory Morse, 54; Craig Sterken/Shutterstock.com, 54; Jim West/Alamy, 55; Cynthia Lindow/Alamy, 55; Gary Paul Lewis/Shutterstock.com, 56; Jess Merrill/Alamy, 58; Jess Merrill/Alamy, 60; David Hume Kennerly/Getty Images, 62; Ethan Miller/Getty Images, 62; David Ryder/Getty Images, 62; AP Photo/Paul Sancya, 64; Daniel Teetor/Alamy, 66; Ilene MacDonald/Alamy, 67; Maria Dryfhout/Shutterstock.com, 68; Wolfgang Kaehler/Superstock, 68; Wally Eberhart/Getty Images, 69; rscreativeworks/Shutterstock.com, 69; Ildi Papp/Shutterstock. com, 70; Chris Raboir Sports Photography/Alamy, 72; Christopher Santoro, 74; Jim West/Alamy, 75; Anne Kitzman/Shutterstock.com, 75; Christopher Santoro, 76; Universal Images Group Limited/Alamy, 76.

Printed in the United States of America

MICHIGAN
CONTENTS

A Quick Look at Michigan 4

1. The Great Lakes State 7
Michigan County Map 10
Michigan Population by County 11
10 Key Sites 14
10 Key Plants and Animals 20

2. From the Beginning 23
The Native People 26
Making a Beaded Keychain 30
10 Key Cities 34
10 Key Dates in State History 43

3. The People 45
10 Key People 48
10 Key Events 54

4. How the Government Works 57
Political Figures from Michigan 62
You Can Make a Difference 63

5. Making a Living 65
10 Key Industries 68
Recipe for Easy Apple Cobbler 70

Michigan State Map 74
Michigan Map Skills 75
State Flag, Seal, and Song 76
Glossary 77
More About Michigan 78
Index 79

A QUICK LOOK AT
STATEHOOD: JANUARY 26, 1837

State Tree: White Pine

The white pine was named Michigan's official state tree in 1955. It can grow to heights of more than 100 feet (30 meters) and can have a trunk that is more than 4 feet (1.2 m) wide. This tree has become a symbol of lumbering in Michigan. Among the animals that live in white pines is the bald eagle.

State Bird: American Robin

Recognized by its dark coloring and red chest, the robin can be found all over Michigan—in backyards, gardens, fields, and forests. The birds nest in the spring and early summer, with females laying up to seven delicate blue eggs that hatch in about two weeks. The robin was made the official state bird in 1931.

State Flower: Apple Blossom

Flowering on the branches of apple trees, the apple blossom has large, pink-and-white petals and green leaves. It is very fragrant and has a sweet, pleasing smell. Apples are an important crop for the state, and this flower was officially chosen in 1897.

MICHIGAN
POPULATION: 9,883,640

State Fish: Brook Trout

Brook trout thrive in the cold lakes, streams, and ponds of Michigan. In late summer or early fall, they lay their eggs on the gravel floor of small streams. Michigan lawmakers in 1965 named the trout as the official state fish. In 1988, lawmakers specified the brook trout as the official fish.

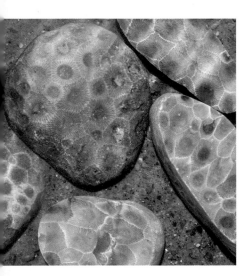

State Stone: Petoskey Stone

These stones found near the town of Petoskey are the fossil remains of coral that formed more than 350 million years ago, when the region was under a saltwater sea. In 1965, it was named the state stone. The six-sided coral polyps, named *Hexagonaria percarinata*, were spread across the northern Lower Peninsula by glaciers.

State Wildflower: Dwarf Lake Iris

This attractive plant, which has blue or violet flowers, was made the official state wildflower in 1998. Dwarf lake irises grow well in moist and sandy soil and are found along the shores of Lake Huron and Lake Michigan.

Miners' Castle is one of the many beautiful rock formations that line the 40-mile (64-kilometer) Pictured Rocks National Lakeshore on Lake Superior in the Upper Peninsula.

The Great Lakes State

Michigan is home to many bodies of freshwater. There are more than eleven thousand lakes in Michigan, and streams flow for more than 36,000 miles (58,000 kilometers) within its borders. Michigan is the only state that borders four of the five Great Lakes. In fact, someone could stand anywhere in Michigan and be within 6 miles (10 km) of a lake or stream or within 85 miles (135 km) of one of the Great Lakes.

Massive glaciers, or sheets of ice, shaped the Michigan landscape. These glaciers moved slowly across the land beginning more than two million years ago. As the glaciers—some as thick as 1 mile (1.6 km) or more—crept along, they carved out Michigan's geographical features. The Great Lakes and Michigan's valleys, rivers, hills, ridges, and flatlands are all mainly a result of glacial movement. The last glaciers began to melt about fourteen thousand years ago, leaving behind soil, pebbles, and boulders.

Michigan Borders

North:	Lake Superior
	Lake Huron
	Canada
South:	Indiana
	Ohio
East:	Canada
	Lake Huron
	Lake Erie
West:	Lake Michigan
	Wisconsin

Michigan has a land area of 56,804 square miles (147,121 square kilometers), making it the twenty-second-largest state in the United States in terms of land area. It has such a large water area—39,912 square miles (103,372 sq km)—that its total area is 96,716 square miles (250,493 sq km). It ranks as the eleventh-largest state in total area.

Michigan is made up of two **peninsulas**: the Upper Peninsula and the Lower Peninsula. A peninsula is a piece of land that juts into bodies of water. The state has eighty-three counties in its two peninsulas.

The Upper Peninsula

Most of the rabbit-shaped Upper Peninsula is made up of forests. Farms are spread out across the region. The cities of the Upper Peninsula generally have smaller populations than the ones in the Lower Peninsula. Marquette, located on Lake Superior, is the Upper Peninsula's most-populated city.

Sault Sainte Marie is another important city in the Upper Peninsula. Located in the east near the Canadian border, it is Michigan's oldest city. Because it sits on the shores of the Saint Marys River—which connects Lake Huron and Lake Superior—Sault Sainte Marie has long been important to the state's economy.

In the northwestern section of the Upper Peninsula are the tree-covered Porcupine Mountains. The native Ojibwe, or Chippewa, people called the mountains "Kag-wadjiw," which means Porcupine Mountains, because they look like a porcupine rising out of

Lake of the Clouds is located in the Porcupine Mountains Wilderness State Park. It covers 133 acres (54 hectares).

Isle Royale National Park, an island in Lake Superior, provides a home for moose and many other kinds of wildlife.

Lake Superior. The mountain range is 12 miles (19 km) long and is located in Ontonagon and Gogebic Counties. Some residents refer to them as "The Porkies."

The Upper Peninsula is also home to many national sites that are valued for their natural beauty. Pictured Rocks National Lakeshore is located on the peninsula's Lake Superior shore. Isle Royale National Park is a large island in the lake. Hiawatha National Forest, Seney National Wildlife Refuge, and Ottawa National Forest are also popular places for hikers, campers, and sightseers. Already open for use is much of the Upper Peninsula portion of the North Country National Scenic Trail, which is being assembled by the National Park Service in the northern United States. (Segments of the trail in the Lower Peninsula are also open.)

The Lower Peninsula

The Upper and Lower Peninsulas are connected only by a great human-made bridge that stretches over 5 miles (8 km) of water called the **Straits** of Mackinac. (The straits connect Lakes Michigan and Huron.) The Lower Peninsula is often described as being shaped like a mitten. The land is a mixture of forests, hills, flatlands, and sand **dunes**.

Some of the Lower Peninsula's most famous natural features are its sand dunes. A sand dune is a ridge or hill made up of sand. The sand in these dunes consists mostly of the mineral quartz. Most of the sand was created when heavy glaciers passed over the area and crushed the rock. Winds and moving water formed the dunes. The sand dunes in

MICHIGAN
COUNTY MAP

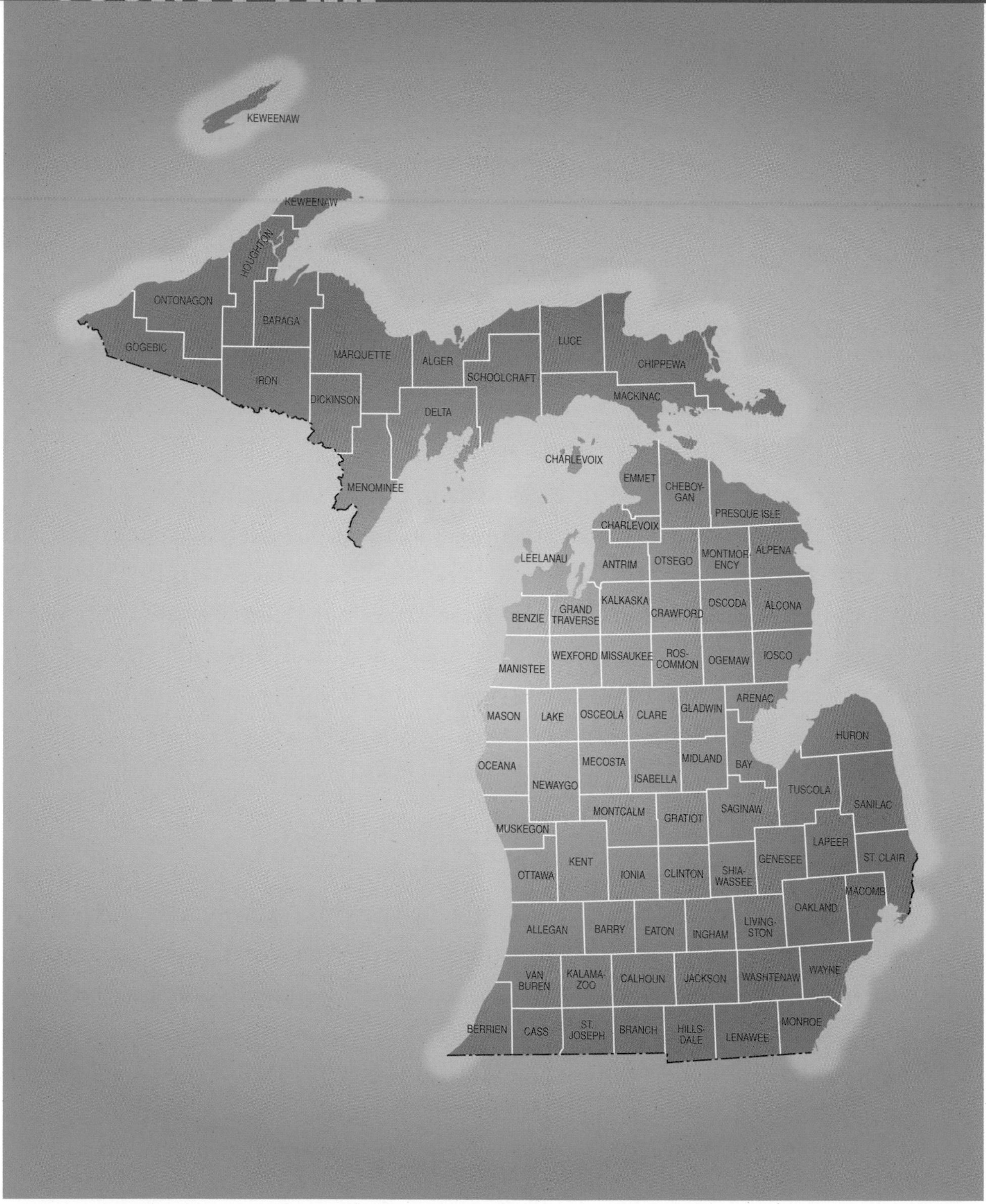

MICHIGAN

POPULATION BY COUNTY

County	Population	County	Population	County	Population
Alcona County	10,942	Gratiot County	42,476	Missaukee County	14,849
Alger County	9,601	Hillsdale County	46,688	Monroe County	152,021
Allegan County	111,408	Houghton County	36,628	Montcalm County	63,342
Alpena County	29,598	Huron County	33,118	Montmorency County	9,765
Antrim County	23,580	Ingham County	280,895	Muskegon County	172,188
Arenac County	15,899	Ionia County	63,905	Newaygo County	48,460
Baraga County	8,860	Iosco County	25,887	Oakland County	1,202,362
Barry County	59,173	Iron County	11,817	Oceana County	26,570
Bay County	107,771	Isabella County	70,311	Ogemaw County	21,699
Benzie County	17,525	Jackson County	160,248	Ontonagon County	6,780
Berrien County	156,813	Kalamazoo County	250,331	Osceola County	23,528
Branch County	45,248	Kalkaska County	17,153	Oscoda County	8,640
Calhoun County	136,146	Kent County	602,622	Otsego County	24,164
Cass County	52,293	Keweenaw County	2,156	Ottawa County	263,801
Charlevoix County	25,949	Lake County	11,539	Presque Isle County	13,376
Cheboygan County	26,152	Lapeer County	88,319	Roscommon County	24,449
Chippewa County	38,520	Leelanau County	21,708	Saginaw County	200,169
Clare County	30,926	Lenawee County	99,892	St. Clair County	163,040
Clinton County	75,382	Livingston County	180,967	Saint Joseph County	61,295
Crawford County	14,074	Luce County	6,631	Sanilac County	43,114
Delta County	37,069	Mackinac County	11,113	Schoolcraft County	8,485
Dickinson County	26,168	Macomb County	840,978	Shiawassee County	70,648
Eaton County	107,759	Manistee County	24,733	Tuscola County	55,729
Emmet County	32,694	Marquette County	67,077	Van Buren County	76,258
Genesee County	425,790	Mason County	28,705	Washtenaw County	344,791
Gladwin County	25,692	Mecosta County	42,798	Wayne County	1,820,584
Gogebic County	16,427	Menominee County	24,029	Wexford County	32,735
Grand Traverse County	86,986	Midland County	83,629		

Source: US Bureau of the Census, 2010

The massive Sleeping Bear Dunes National Lakeshore includes bluffs that rise up to 450 feet (137 meters) above Lake Michigan.

Michigan are considered to be one of the great wonders of the world, and Michigan has the world's largest group of freshwater sand dunes. Sand dunes are located along much of the shore of the Great Lakes, but the state's best-known dunes are on the Lake Michigan shore in the western part of the Lower Peninsula. There are more than 275,000 acres (111,000 hectares) of sand dunes in Michigan. The Sleeping Bear Dunes National Lakeshore can even be seen from outer space. In open areas of the dunes, the surface temperature of the sand can be as hot as 180 degrees Fahrenheit (80 degrees Celsius).

The sand dunes are home to plants and animals that might not be found in other parts of Michigan. Birds and insects migrating during the year use the dunes as a landmark. Sand dunes are also home to eastern box turtles. These turtles are few in number, and experts worry that they may someday die out. Plants such as marram grass protect the dunes by sheltering them from the wind. The root systems of the grass also help stabilize the sand dunes from beneath. Without these plants, the dunes could blow away with strong winds.

Other treasured natural sites recognized by the federal government in the Lower Peninsula include Manistee National Forest, Huron National Forest, Thunder Bay National Marine Sanctuary and Underwater Preserve, Michigan Islands National Wildlife Refuge, and Shiawassee National Wildlife Refuge.

The Detroit River International Wildlife Refuge—the first international wildlife refuge in North America—is a joint effort between the United States and Canada. The refuge was established in 2001.

The Upper Tahquamenon Falls are more than 200 feet (60 m) wide and drop almost 50 feet (15 m).

The Great Lakes

The five Great Lakes are Lake Superior, Lake Michigan, Lake Huron, Lake Erie, and Lake Ontario. The only Great Lake that does not touch the borders of Michigan is Lake Ontario. The lakes have helped shape Michigan's shores, which feature many bays and coves. Michigan's land also includes islands surrounded by the lakes' waters.

Michigan also has many important inland bodies of water. The Upper Peninsula has rivers such as the Menominee, Whitefish, Manistique, Tahquamenon, and Escanaba. The Saint Joseph, Kalamazoo, Saginaw, Muskegon, and Au Sable Rivers are just some of the large waterways crossing through parts of the Lower Peninsula. Michigan's longest river is the Grand River. It starts in the south-central part of the state and flows toward the west, eventually emptying into Lake Michigan. The rushing waters of many of the state's streams and rivers form striking waterfalls. There are nearly two hundred named waterfalls within Michigan's borders, almost all of them in the Upper Peninsula. The Upper Tahquamenon Falls rank as one of the largest waterfalls east of the Mississippi River.

The Michigan Wetlands

Some of Michigan's best natural resources are its wetlands. Wetlands are areas of land close to water with a lot of moisture in the soil. Sometimes they may even be covered with shallow water. Examples of wetlands include swamps, bogs, and marshes. Michigan wetlands are found especially often along the coasts of the Great Lakes. These are called coastal wetlands.

The wetlands provide a unique habitat for the plants and animals that thrive there. Flowers such as milkweed and boneset attract butterflies such as monarchs, swallowtails, and fritillaries. Chorus frogs and tree frogs make the wetlands their temporary homes while they raise their tadpoles. Tall grasses provide shade for insects and animals. The

1. Belle Isle Park

Located on an island in the Detroit River, this 985-acre (398 ha) park contains a variety of attractions. There is an aquarium, a conservatory, the famous James Scott Memorial Fountain, and other educational and recreational opportunities.

2. Detroit Institute of Arts

More than one hundred galleries house a diverse collection of art from throughout the world. Included is a collection from Africa and an exhibit of African-American art. Works are from prehistory to the twenty-first century.

3. Gilmore Car Museum

The 90 acres (36 ha) of this museum in Hickory Corners display a collection of more than three hundred vintage motorcycles and automobiles. You can eat at a 1940s-style diner, see a collection of toy cars, and view historic exhibits.

4. Great Lakes Shipwreck Museum

The waters of eastern Lake Superior in the Upper Peninsula have claimed many ships over the centuries. The most famous of these is the *Edmund Fitzgerald*. Learn about these disasters at this seasonal museum at Whitefish Point.

5. Henry Ford Museum

This celebration of imagination in Dearborn brings to life American ideas and innovation. Henry Ford is associated with automobiles, but this museum features airplanes, artwork, exhibits, and stories of all the innovations that built the US economy.

Belle Isle Park

Gilmore Car Museum

Great Lakes Shipwreck Museum

6. Kalamazoo Air Zoo

This science center allows people to ride in flight simulators, get a close look at historic aircraft, view artwork that celebrates flight, learn the history of flight while riding an indoor ferris wheels, and see other educational exhibits.

7. Mackinac Island

Hiking, biking, boating, kayaking, carriage rides, entertainment, and relaxation are all features of this beautiful resort. Fort Mackinac is one of many historic locations. It was taken by the British in 1812.

8. Petoskey

This small town and its neighbor, Bay View, sit in the northwestern part of the Lower Peninsula. Bay View has Victorian cottages that are designated National Historic Landmarks. Petoskey stone, the state stone, can be found on the beaches. Boyne Mountain Resort is nearby.

9. Pictured Rocks National Lakeshore

The 40 miles (64 km) of this magnificent stretch of the Lake Superior shore brings you into contact with sand dunes, sandstone cliffs, waterfalls, beaches, and lakes. There are more than 100 miles (160 km) of hiking trails, and you can kayak under the cliffs.

10. Traverse City

Beaches, great restaurants, nearby Sleeping Bear Dunes, and other attractions bring people to this bayside city near Lake Michigan. Among the activities are hiking, biking, boating, golf, a film festival, a hockey tournament, and fall leaf peeping.

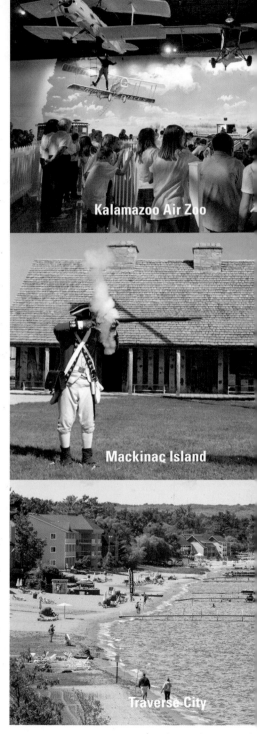

Kalamazoo Air Zoo

Mackinac Island

Traverse City

Fall weather brings brilliant colors to wooded areas all over Michigan. Peak dates start in early October in the Upper Peninsula and in late October near Ohio.

wetlands provide water, food, and a place to rest as ducks, geese, and other birds migrate south for the winter or north for the summer.

The Changing Seasons

Michigan's **climate** is affected by the Great Lakes. The winds off the water help cool temperatures in summer and keep them a little warmer in the winter. In the summer, temperatures usually range from about 50°F to about 83°F (10°C to 28°C). The Upper Peninsula usually experiences cooler temperatures than the Lower Peninsula. Michigan does not often suffer damaging summer storms, although tornadoes occasionally strike, especially in the southern part of the Lower Peninsula.

Many people especially enjoy Michigan in the fall. The temperatures are usually neither too cold nor too hot, and the leaves on many of the state's trees change colors to striking oranges, yellows, and reds. By November, however, temperatures begin to drop and snow starts to fall.

The winter months in Michigan are chilly, with temperatures usually between about 3°F and 36°F (between −16°C and 2°C). Michigan is one of several states on the Great Lakes that experience lake-effect snow. The water of the Great Lakes is often warmer than the air during the coldest months. When cold, dry arctic air passes over the lakes, it is warmed. Water evaporates into the dry air, and large amounts of snow fall when the air hits land. This is referred to as lake-effect snow. In January 1982, 129.5 inches (328.9 centimeters)—more than 10 feet (3 m)—of snow fell on Copper Harbor near the tip of the Upper Peninsula's Keweenaw Peninsula. This is the most on record for any month at any

Mark the Date

The North Country Scenic Trail crosses the Mackinac Bridge. However, people may cross that bridge on foot only during the annual walk. Tens of thousands of people participate each year.

The efforts of conservationists have allowed gray wolves to make a comeback in Michigan.

weather station in the state. But most years are not like 1982, and most places in Michigan are not like Copper Harbor. The average annual amount of snow that falls in Michigan ranges from roughly 40 inches (100 cm) in the southeastern part of the Lower Peninsula to more than 200 inches (500 cm) in the Copper Harbor region.

It is not uncommon to have snow in April. Spring in Michigan can be rainy and very wet, but the promise of summer helps keep many Michiganders in good spirits.

Name Calling

Only one wolverine has been spotted in Michigan since the early 1800s. It was seen in 2004 and died in 2010. No one knows why one of Michigan's names was the Wolverine State. One theory is that during the Toledo War in 1835, Ohioans called Michiganders wolverines because they were so ornery.

Wildlife

Michigan has a wide variety of plants, flowers, fish, and other wildlife. About 53 percent of the land in the state is covered with forests. Tall pines, firs, cedars, maples, oaks, and birches are among the trees growing in these forests. Other trees found across the state include hickory, elm, spruce, and aspen.

Hundreds of types of flowers grow in Michigan. Evening primrose, dense blazing star, pale coneflower, rosinweed, milkweed, and smooth aster are a few examples. Some plants, such as pale agoseris, are found only in a few areas. Pale agoseris usually occurs in grassy areas more common in the Great Plains of the west-central United States. But it also grows in the northern part of Michigan's Lower Peninsula, which has open grassy areas like those found in the Great Plains.

Michigan's forests are home to deer, snowshoe hares, ducks, woodchucks, coyotes, badgers, bald eagles, black bears, and bobcats. White-tailed deer are found in every county, and in 1997 this deer was picked as the official state game mammal. ("Game" means animals that are hunted.) Moose and gray wolves (also called timber wolves) are found on Isle Royale and have also been seen in the forests of the Upper Peninsula mainland. Michigan's animals also include bats, beavers, raccoons, skunks, and rabbits.

Many kinds of birds make their homes in Michigan's trees. These include eagles, falcons, owls, hummingbirds, wrens, sparrows, doves, and cardinals. Other Michigan birds live in the state's wetlands, sand dunes, or grasslands. Some of these birds are herons, egrets, and sandpipers.

Michigan's waters are filled with fish, amphibians, and other water creatures. Frogs, toads, and salamanders live in Michigan's moist areas. Fish such as lake herring, carp, catfish, perch, bass, salmon, sturgeon, and muskellunge swim through the rivers, streams, and lakes.

Endangered Animals

An endangered species is a type of animal or plant that exists in such small numbers that it is in danger of becoming extinct and disappearing forever. Species may become endangered when their natural environment is damaged or destroyed as a result of natural disasters, human interference, or pollution. A species's continued existence may also be threatened by disease.

The Indiana bat is one endangered species found in Michigan. This mammal has grayish-brown fur and a pink underbelly. It is about 3 inches (7.6 cm) long and has a wingspan (the total length from one wingtip to the other when the wings are stretched

The Kirtland's warbler is endangered due to a lack of its natural habitat.

out) of 9 to 11 inches (23 to 28 cm). These bats hibernate throughout the winter in caves or abandoned mines. During the spring and summer months, they live near streams, under loose bark in trees. Fewer than four hundred thousand of these bats remain in the United States. Federal law makes it illegal for humans to interfere with or harm in any way endangered species such as these little creatures.

Another endangered animal in Michigan is the Kirtland's warbler, a rare bird that usually mates in Michigan. It is known for its loud song. These birds nest mostly in jack pine trees in a few Michigan counties in the northern parts of the Lower Peninsula. Jack pine trees depend on natural wildfires to destroy old trees, making room for young jack pines to grow. Since natural wildfires are being prevented to protect human communities, the birds have fewer young jack pines in which to live. The US Fish and Wildlife Service placed the warbler on the endangered species list in 1973. Efforts by scientists in Michigan and elsewhere to plant more young jack pines have led to an increase in the number of Kirtland's warblers.

There were twenty-seven plant and animal species listed as threatened or endangered in Michigan in 2015, including the gray wolf.

The Michigan Department of Natural Resources conserves and protects the state's natural resources by doing research to prevent problems, teaching residents about how to protect the environment, and taking action when a problem arises. By protecting the environment, Michiganders ensure their land will be healthy for future generations.

★10★KEY PLANTS AND ANIMALS

1. Black Bear

Black bears are most common in the Upper Peninsula. Female black bears weigh between 100 and 250 pounds (between 45 and 113 kilograms), and adult males can weigh from 150 to 400 pounds (68 to 180 kg).

Black Bear

2. Cardinal Flower

The cardinal flower is found along river and stream banks, along the shores of lakes, and in swamps. This plant's name comes from its ruby-red flowers. They bloom in late summer and early fall, and they often attract hummingbirds.

Cardinal Flower

3. Four-Toed Salamander

The four-toed salamander can be found throughout most of Michigan in boggy ponds, creeks, and forests. These amphibians measure 2 to 4 four inches (5 to 10 cm) long. They eat insects, spiders, and worms.

4. Green Darner Dragonfly

The green darner dragonfly is one of the largest and most spectacular of all types, or species, of dragonfly. Green darners have silvery wings, a deep-emerald-colored throat, and a blue belly with a streak of deep red.

Green Darner Dragonfly

5. Jack Pine

Jack pines thrive in the drier parts of Michigan. Found on sand dunes and in regions with sandy soil, the trees are often short and tend to have a crooked trunk. Michigan's lumber industry harvests jack pines for use as building materials and for making paper.

6. Moose

Extensive logging and hunting nearly eliminated this large mammal that used to be found throughout much of Michigan. Restoration efforts began in the 1930s, and with the help of citizens, populations in the Upper Peninsula have been increasing.

7. Short-Eared Owl

Short-eared owls live in grasslands, and unlike other kinds of owls, they hunt both during the day and at night. They nest in clumps of plants or at the base of shrubs in Michigan's grasslands. A typical nest might contain between five and seven eggs.

Short-Eared Owl

Whitefish

8. White Birch

The Anishnaabe people, who are indigenous to Michigan, used the bark of the white birch to make canoes, to cover their wigwams, and to make baskets. Insects and diseases are threatening these trees.

9. Whitefish

The whitefish is a mainstay of the waters of the Great Lakes and is a favorite food in Michigan. Native Americans have sought this sub-member of the salmon family for centuries. Whitefish average 2 to 4 pounds (0.9 to 1.8 kg).

10. White-Tailed Deer

This common animal is the state's official game animal. It has provided food for the people of Michigan for thousands of years, and is a favorite of hunters today. The deer's white tail flips up as a warning to others if danger is detected.

White-Tailed Deer

William Lamprecht painted *Father Marquette and the Indians* in 1869. The priest started his explorations in Michigan.

From the Beginning

Around 12,000 BCE, the glaciers that once covered the region that is now Michigan began retreating. This process took many centuries. Scientists believe that humans first started living in the area roughly around 10,000 BCE. These early people are called Paleo-Indians ("ancient Indians"). They used stone tools and hunted animals with spears. They also gathered plants for food.

Copper People and Mound Builders

The period lasting from about 8000 BCE to about 1000 BCE is called the Archaic period. The peoples living then developed new tools using stone and wood. Large deposits of copper were found on Isle Royale and the Keweenaw Peninsula. Copper mining began. The people who made and used copper tools and other objects are sometimes called the Old Copper people. Things made of copper and other materials dating from the later parts of the Archaic period have been found in places other than where the materials originated. This suggests that trade activity was already going on.

The Archaic period was followed, beginning about 1000 BCE, by the Woodland period. People in this period began planting gardens, making pottery, and building mounds of earth over graves. Sometime in the middle of the Woodland period, between around 300 BCE

A museum display shows the way scientists believe Native Americans mined copper.

Trade Name

The Ottawa relied more heavily on trading than did other tribes in Michigan. In fact their name comes from a word meaning "to trade."

and around 500 CE, a new group of people arrived from the south. Historians refer to this new group of people as the Hopewell.

The Hopewell people built very large burial mounds, some of which remain. Along with their dead, the Hopewell buried tools, pottery, and other goods. Enormous amounts of dirt were piled on graves, forming the mounds. It is also possible that the mounds, under which as many as twenty people might be buried, served a religious purpose. The Hopewell seem to have been great traders. Scientists have found in their mounds not only objects made of copper and other materials from the region but also objects using materials from very distant places—for example, shells from the Gulf of Mexico and freshwater pearls from the Mississippi River valley.

One of the best-known groups of Hopewell burial mounds is the Norton Mounds, in what is now Grand Rapids. Remains of pottery and tools found in the mounds are on display at the Van Andel Museum Center in Grand Rapids. No one knows what happened to the Hopewell people. They may have moved away or joined other groups.

Three Fires

When the first Europeans arrived in the region in the early seventeenth century, three of the most important Native American groups in what is now Michigan were the Ojibwe, Ottawa (also called Odawa), and Potawatomi. They had an **alliance** called the Council of Three Fires. The members of the three groups were known as the People of the Three Fires. They helped each other protect their land, and they shared hunting, farming, and craft skills.

The Huron were another Native American group in the region that now includes Michigan. They lived in **longhouses**. They grew beans, corn, and squash and also hunted and fished. Their population before the Europeans arrived was estimated at about thirty thousand. By 1640, they were thought to number fewer than ten thousand—as a result of disease and war.

The French Arrive

The first Europeans to reach what is now Michigan were the French. They began coming to the area in the early seventeenth century as they looked for a so-called Northwest Passage. This was a waterway that, it was thought, would cut across all of North America, making it possible to travel from the Atlantic Ocean to Asia. In 1618, the French explorer

Native Americans, especially the Ottawa, swapped furs for goods with European traders.

The Native People

Native Americans have a long history in Michigan. Some tribes were there long before the arrival of European explorers, and some were driven there as white settlers moved into their lands to the east. The original tribes can be divided into those living in the Upper Peninsula and those living in the Lower Peninsula, though they lived in neighboring regions as well. For example, the Ojibwe and the Menominee lived in the Upper Peninsula, and the Menominee had a large presence—and still do—in Wisconsin. The Potawatomi were the largest tribe in the Lower Peninsula.

The climate and the geography does not vary much from place to place in Michigan, so it is not surprising that the tribes in the region lived in the same way. They hunted for large and small game, such as deer, moose, and rabbits, and they fished for walleye, whitefish, and other freshwater species in the region's lakes and rivers. Most of them grew rice, corn, and squash. They wore skins of the animals they hunted, made their homes from bark and mud, and moved villages to follow fish or game.

The Huron, also known as the Wyandot, and the Ottawa migrated to Michigan from what is now New York State, Quebec, and eastern Ontario. All the tribes in the region suffered when white settlers arrived. The land closest to the waterways used for transportation was taken. Diseases brought by whites killed two out of every three Native Americans in the region in the 1700s. Whites had seized half of the land in the Lower Peninsula by 1820. Many Native Americans were resettled west of the Mississippi River into areas known as Indian Territory.

There are eleven federally recognized tribes living on reservations in Michigan today, although less than 1 percent of the state's population is Native American. The tribes include branches of the Ottawa, Chippewa, Huron, and the Potawatomi. The People of the Three Fires – the Potawatomi, the Ottawa, and the Chippewa or Ojibwe, are the major tribes. They banded together to form the Three Fires Council.

Spotlight on the Potawatomi

Many groups of Potawatomi were removed from their land between 1834 and 1842. Some avoided removal, and three of them remain in Michigan today—the Huron Potawatomi live in the south-central part of the state, the Pokagon Potawatomi live in the southwest region and bordering northern Indiana, and the Hannahville Potawatomi live in the Upper Peninsula.

The Potawatomi used the white bark of the birch tree to cover their wigwams and lodges

Government: The Potawatomi communities were called tribes. They were independent, and each had its own chief, who was usually the leader of a leading clan. Today the chief is the leader of an entire band and is elected by members of the band.

Homes: The Potawatomi built wigwams, which were dome-shaped, and rectangular lodges. They covered both with birch bark.

Dress: The men wore deerskin shirts, leggings, and breechcloths. The women wore long dresses made of deerskin. The men wore leather headbands with a few feathers sticking up out of the headband.

Games: The men and boys played lacrosse. The girls played a less violent form of lacrosse called double shinny. The ball was stuffed with fur and covered with deerskin, or it was made of wood. The lacrosse stick was made from a sapling that was looped at the tip and covered with netting made of leather.

Art: The Potawatomi Weave is a style of bead embroidery named for the tribe. The tribe was also know for its quill embroidery and its basketry. It also made wampum out of beads of white and purple shell, and made wampum belts decorated with beads in a way to tell a story.

Étienne Brûlé landed at what is now Sault Sainte Marie. He is believed to be the first European to set foot in the area we call Michigan. No waterway such as the Northwest Passage existed, but French traders kept returning to the area. They wanted the pelts—or fur—of foxes, minks, and beavers. These pelts were very valuable in Europe and were used to make warm clothing and hats.

By 1650, a number of French fur traders had traveled the Saint Lawrence River to the Great Lakes to trade goods for furs with the Native Americans. The French traded a variety of European goods for the fur pelts: cloth, iron pots, hatchets, guns, and alcohol. In the beginning, Native Americans welcomed fur traders and taught them to speak their languages and to track animals.

French Catholic missionaries also began coming to the area in the seventeenth century. Missionaries are people who travel to spread their beliefs and way of life. The most famous French missionary in the region was Jacques Marquette. Marquette is also considered one of the great explorers of North America. He arrived in Quebec, Canada, in 1666. There he worked among the Native Americans, learning some of their languages and teaching them about Christianity. In 1668, Marquette founded a mission at a place that was given the name Sault Sainte Marie. This is considered the first European settlement in the land that makes up Michigan.

In 1671, Marquette established the St. Ignace mission on the north shore of the Straits of Mackinac between the Upper and Lower Peninsulas. The region's first French military fort, Fort de Buade, was built at St. Ignace around 1690. Traders called the **outpost** Michilimackinac, the Ojibwe name for the area. The fort was manned for only a few years. In 1715, a new fort called Fort Michilimackinac was built on the northern tip of the Lower Peninsula. It became a busy fur-trading center.

An important role was played by Antoine Laumet de la Mothe, sieur de Cadillac. In 1694, he took command of Fort de Buade. Cadillac later decided that the French needed to build another post farther south, to protect the area against the English, who had already colonized much of North America's East Coast. Cadillac proposed building the new fort on the waterway between Lakes Huron and Erie. The French called this waterway

Explorer and missionary priest Jacques Marquette established friendly relations with Native Americans and learned their languages.

Changing Hands

The flags of four nations have flown over what is now Michigan. First Spain, then France, Great Britain, and the United States.

Détroit ("The Strait"). The French king, Louis XIV, agreed, and in 1701, Cadillac and about one hundred people founded Fort Ponchartrain. The settlement at Fort Ponchartrain would become the city of Detroit. The portion of the waterway by Detroit is now called the Detroit River.

The British Take Control

Until the eighteenth century, the French had the only European settlements in the region. But the profits from the fur trade attracted the British. In 1754, war broke out in North America between France and Great Britain. The fighting spread to Europe in 1756 and then to other parts of the world. In North America, where the struggle is referred to as

Making a Beaded Keychain

The Native Americans of Michigan are highly skilled at using beads to decorate their clothing and some items they use. Some of their beading patterns are complex, such as the Potawatomi Weave. By following these simple instructions, you can make a beaded decoration to hang on your key ring.

What You Need

One leather strip, 6 to 8 inches (15 to 20 cm) long
Wooden beads with holes big enough for the leather strip

What To Do

- Fold the leather strip in half.
- Tie a small knot near the closed end so there is a loop above the knot.
- Starting at the open end, string beads in your desired pattern. Make sure you pass both pieces of the leather strip through the beads. Leave 1 inch (2.5 cm) at the bottom of the strip.
- Tie another knot at the open end of keychain. The knot should be right next to the last bead.
- Thread your key ring through the loop, and you have your own, unique keychain.

the French and Indian War (1754–1763), Britain and France fought over who would control what is now the Midwest and parts of Canada, including the land that makes up Michigan. The war ended with a British victory in 1763, and most of North America east of the Mississippi River came under British control.

As the British took over, some Native American leaders, including an Ottawa chief called Pontiac, felt that the time had come when the Europeans' presence could no longer be tolerated. The Native Americans feared the loss of their hunting grounds to British settlers. Also, the British paid less for furs than the French had paid, and were less welcoming to Native American traders. Moreover, the British were no longer willing to promote good relations by supplying the Native Americans with food, guns, and clothing. Pontiac gathered a number of tribes from the Great Lakes area and planned a surprise attack against the British. This would later be called Pontiac's Rebellion.

In May 1763, Pontiac and his warriors surrounded and attacked the British fort at Detroit, and other warriors began attacking forts and outposts elsewhere. The Native American warriors succeeded in capturing several British forts, but the British in Detroit learned of the attack and kept control of the fort there for nearly seven months. Eventually, Pontiac and his men were forced to give up. Their siege of Detroit was the last major confrontation between Native Americans and European settlers in what is now Michigan.

After the French and Indian War, Britain needed money to pay for the costs of war. The British government sought to impose new taxes on its American colonies. Hoping to avoid new conflicts with the Native Americans, Britain tried to stop the colonists from settling in much of the region it took from France. The British government also set up other rules and laws that the colonists did not like. These actions led many colonists to want independence from Britain and eventually contributed to the outbreak of the American Revolution in 1775.

A New Nation

Most of the fighting of the American Revolution (1775–1783) took place on the East Coast of North America. To help keep their position in what is now Michigan, the British abandoned the wooden Fort Michilimackinac on the south shore of the Straits of Mackinac and built a strong new stone fort on Mackinac Island, located in Lake Huron

Captain Oliver Perry, painted escaping to the brig *Niagara* after his ship was heavily damaged, won the Battle of Lake Erie, driving the British out of Detroit and all of Michigan.

just outside the straits. This fort, called Fort Mackinac, was built around 1780. In 1783, the Treaty of Paris was signed, officially ending the war with America independent. According to the treaty, the Americans gained control of the land that would become Michigan. But the British did not surrender Fort Mackinac until 1796.

In 1787, Congress passed a law organizing the large area northwest of the Ohio River that had been received from Britain. This area—called the Northwest **Territory**—would eventually become the states of Michigan, Ohio, Indiana, Illinois, and Wisconsin, as well as part of Minnesota. The law was called the Northwest Ordinance. It said that a region within the Northwest Territory could apply for statehood once its population reached sixty thousand. In 1805, Congress established the Territory of Michigan, which included present-day Michigan along with Wisconsin and part of Minnesota. But it would still be many years before Michigan was eligible for statehood.

The new United States struggled against the British one more time during the War of 1812. The Americans were angry because the British often kidnapped American sailors and made them work on British ships. These kidnappings were called impressments.

The Americans also discovered that the British were supplying Native American groups with weapons and encouraging them to attack American settlements. In the early stages of the war, the British quickly captured Fort Mackinac and Detroit, and for a year or so, they controlled Michigan again. But the American navy achieved an important victory on Lake Erie in 1813. The Battle of Lake Erie forced the British out of the Michigan Territory for good.

Michigan Becomes a State

Many people began to settle in the Michigan Territory in the early nineteenth century. The Erie Canal was completed in New York State in 1825. It linked the Great Lakes with the Atlantic Ocean. This waterway bypassed Niagara Falls and provided a quick route between the eastern states and the lands of the former Northwest Territory. Transporting goods and people to Michigan no longer required a difficult trip overland. This helped draw settlers to the fertile farmland that Michigan provided. The Michigan Territory's

Voters take part in the first election after Michigan became a state. It was held in 1837.

1. Detroit: population 713,777

Motor City is the center of the US automobile industry and the home of Motown Records, which popularized soul music. The city was founded in 1701 and exchanged hands in wars several times due to the importance of its location.

2. Grand Rapids: population 188,040

For a mid-sized city, Grand Rapids has some big-time attractions. Among them are the renowed Frederik Meijer Gardens and Sculpture Park (*lower left*), the Meyer May House that was designed by Frank Lloyd Wright, and the Gerald R. Ford Presidential Museum.

3. Warren: population 134,056

The largest suburb of Detroit employs many people in automobile manufacturing and in the military. Warren was home to rapper Eminem, Hall of Fame pitcher John Smoltz, rocker Mitch Ryder, and hockey star Doug Weight.

4. Sterling Heights: population 129,699

The second-largest suburb of Detroit is home to the Polish American Festival, in honor of one of the state's largest ethnic groups. It is known as a safe place to live. Sterlingfest in Dodge Park is known for food, carnival rides, and live music.

5. Lansing: population 114,297

The capital city is located in the center of the bottom half of the Lower Peninsula. It is an important center for education, culture, industry, and government. Michigan State University is located in East Lansing.

Detroit

Grand Rapids

6. Ann Arbor: population 113,934

The home of the University of Michigan is just west of Detroit. The university was moved there in 1837. The city features a series of fairy doors, culture, and attractions such as the Nichols Arboretum.

7. Flint: population 102,434

This manufacturing center has been hit hard by job losses in the auto industry. Left from the time when Flint was prosperous are many museums, including the Flint Institute of Arts, the Sloan Museum, and the Flint Children's Museum.

8. Dearborn: population 98,153

This city is the hometown of Henry Ford and the headquarters of the Ford Motor Company. Many of its residents are descendants of the European immigrants from the nineteenth and twentieth centuries, but many are from Arab countries such as Lebanon.

9. Livonia: population 96,942

This residential suburb sits between Detroit and Ann Arbor. The city owns the Greenmead Historical Park, in which buildings from the early nineteenth century show what life was like on a Michigan farm.

10. Westland: population 84,094

Most of Michigan's people live in suburbs around Detroit. This community is located just south of Livonia. The land was once occupied by the Potawatomi. Many people moved to the area during World War II to help build things for the army.

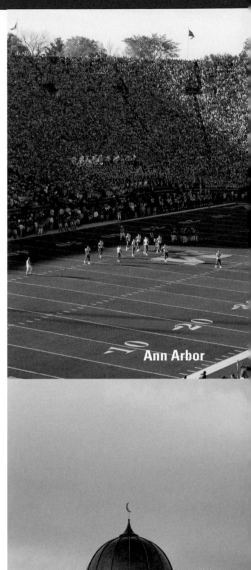

Ann Arbor

Dearborn

 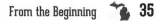

population grew quickly, rising from roughly nine thousand in 1820 to thirty-two thousand in 1830.

A special census found in 1834 that some eighty-six thousand people were living in the Lower Peninsula—more than enough to apply for statehood. Michigan asked to become a state, with its boundaries to include mostly the Lower Peninsula. However, action on statehood was delayed by a conflict over a piece of land called the Toledo Strip. Both Michigan and Ohio claimed this narrow piece of land, which ran along their border from Indiana to Lake Erie. Both Michigan and Ohio sent soldiers to the area. The "Toledo War" ended without serious bloodshed. Congress decided that Ohio would win the Toledo Strip and that Michigan would be granted statehood if it accepted, in exchange, all of the Upper Peninsula. Michigan agreed, and on January 26, 1837, it became the twenty-sixth state. Detroit served as its capital.

At first, Michiganders felt that the Upper Peninsula was a poor trade for the port of Toledo. But the Upper Peninsula provided Michigan with the natural resources that later made it the nation's leader in copper, salt, and iron mining and in lumber production. These industries helped Michigan to prosper and attract many new residents. In 1847, the capital was moved to Lansing, which is closer to the center of the state.

Michigan in the Civil War

In 1861, the Civil War began in the United States. Michigan was one of almost two dozen states, most of them in the northern part of the nation, that sided with the federal government, also referred to as the Union. On the other side were eleven Southern states that seceded (withdrew) from the United States of America and formed the Confederate States of America. One of the issues that divided North and South was slavery. By the beginning of the 1860s, slavery was against the law in most of the North. In the South, there were millions of black slaves working on the region's plantations (large farms).

Slavery was always against the law in the state of Michigan. Antislavery groups, which wanted to see slavery ended throughout the United States, had begun forming in Michigan in the 1830s. Many Michiganders played an important role in helping slaves from the South escape to freedom. A large number of these slaves traveled through Michigan to Canada, where slavery was banned and escaped slaves could not be captured and returned. The Fugitive Slave Acts (passed in 1793 and 1850) allowed escaped slaves to be captured and returned to their owners. Under those laws, many free black people were taken and sold into slavery. **Abolitionists,** people who were against slavery, hid the escaping slaves and provided food, shelter, and money as the slaves journeyed north.

A former slave, Sojourner Truth fought for abolition and for women's rights.

The network of homes, churches, barns, stores, and schools that served as hiding places was called the Underground Railroad. Laura Haviland, a woman from Adrian, Michigan, helped so many slaves that she came to be known as the Superintendent of the Underground Railroad. Another key figure in the Underground Railroad was Sojourner Truth, a former slave who moved to the Battle Creek area in the late 1850s. Detroit, Adrian, and Battle Creek were among the stops on the Underground Railroad.

More than 90,000 men from Michigan served on the side of the Union in the Civil War, including more than 1,600 African Americans and more than 200 Native Americans. Women from Michigan played an important role as well. The Michigan Soldier Relief Association was a group of Michigan women who provided medical care, clothing, food, and newspapers to wounded Michigan soldiers at hospitals in Washington, DC. Historians believe that about fourteen thousand Michigan soldiers died during the war, either in battle or from disease. President Abraham Lincoln acknowledged the contribution Michiganders made to the war, declaring, "Thank God for Michigan."

The Civil War ended in a Union victory in 1865. The eleven states that had seceded were returned to the Union, and the Thirteenth Amendment to the US Constitution, which prohibited slavery throughout the United States, was ratified on December 6, 1865.

Michigan's Industry and the Automobile

After the Civil War, Michigan prospered. The state's enormous supply of trees and minerals helped make it an ideal place to develop different industries. Michigan resources were used to provide the world with steel, ships, iron, stoves, and medicine. All this industry meant there were plenty of jobs in Michigan. Because of this, Michigan's

More than fifteen million Model Ts rolled off Ford's assembly lines between 1908 and 1927.

population continued to grow. The population went from one million in 1870 to more than two million in 1890.

In the following years, pioneering automakers such as Ransom Olds and Henry Ford made Michigan the leader of the country's car industry. Olds, helped by Frank Clark, built an early gasoline-powered automobile in 1896 in Lansing. The following year, the Olds Motor Vehicle Company was formed. It made only a few cars, but in 1899 it became the Olds Motor Works. Most people thought that the idea of automobiles was crazy. The first automobiles were expensive and did not sell well. Nonetheless, Olds's company managed to sell six hundred cars in 1901. Three years later, the figure rose to five thousand. This marked the beginning of **mass production** of gasoline cars in the United States.

Henry Ford, who was born near Detroit, also built a gasoline-powered vehicle in 1896. At the Ford Motor Company, formed in 1903, he adopted on a large scale the use of an **assembly line**, in which each employee puts together one piece of each car. Olds had introduced the assembly-line system into car manufacturing, but Ford expanded it and improved on it. In 1913, he introduced the moving assembly line. Ford's assembly-line system sped up the construction of automobiles, and this reduced the price of the cars. In 1908, Ford's Model T cost $850, which was low compared to other cars of the time. By 1927, Ford had reduced the cost of the Model T to $380. Detroit quickly became the center of the automobile industry.

The Great Depression and Labor Movements

By 1929, Michigan's economy was based on the manufacturing of goods such as cars, refrigerators, and airplanes. But beginning late that year, the United States entered a period of severe economic hardship known as the Great Depression. Many businesses closed, and many people lost their jobs. Like other states, Michigan was hit hard by these economic troubles. With millions of people out of work, the need for Michigan's manufactured items decreased—many people could no longer afford to buy them. By 1933, 46 percent of Michigan's workforce was jobless. Michigan's population fell by nearly 30 percent from 1930 to 1935, as people left the state to try to find jobs elsewhere.

The men and women who were able to keep their jobs often had to work long hours for low wages doing tiresome tasks. Workers formed unions—groups of employees who join together to try to obtain better pay and working conditions. In the 1930s, workers at automobile factories went on strike to protest the poor working conditions. Sometimes these strikes became violent. The nation's first large-scale "sit-down strike" took place in Flint at a General Motors Company factory. Bosses at General Motors refused to talk with the workers' union leaders, so the workers came to work and then sat down, not only refusing to work but also refusing to leave the factory. The strike began at the end of 1936 and lasted forty-four days. The workers were victorious. In 1937, General Motors recognized the workers' union, the United Auto Workers (UAW). This meant that General Motors would negotiate with the union about such matters as pay levels and working conditions. The other automobile manufacturers eventually followed the example of General Motors, and working conditions in the industry improved.

Michigan in World War II

Michigan's economy continued to recover with the onset of World War II (1939–1945). When the United States entered the war in 1941, products from Michigan's factories were

Workers at this plant in Detroit built trucks for the US Army during World War II.

once again in high demand. Auto plants were converted to produce tanks, planes, naval vessels, trucks, and armored cars. Many of the factories that were closed down in the 1930s reopened and ran twenty-four hours a day, providing new jobs for many Michiganders.

Women played an important role in the war effort. With so many men serving in the armed forces, more and more women began working in factories in order to meet the demand for war supplies. To help popularize the idea of women working in factories, the federal government conducted an advertising campaign using the name "Rosie the Riveter," from a popular 1942 song. Rose Monroe, who worked in a factory in Ypsilanti, Michigan, was picked to star in a promotional film for the campaign. Her job included riveting—or connecting—parts for airplanes. Rosie the Riveter became a symbol of women's efforts on the home front during the war.

In Their Own Words

"Any customer can have a car painted any color that he wants as long as it is black."
—Henry Ford

Modern Michigan

In general, the 1960s and 1970s were troubled times for Michigan. Its economy suffered once again as its automobile industry was hurt by

President Barack Obama helped Chrysler and General Motors get through the recession with a financial bailout of the auto industry.

increasing sales of cars from foreign automakers and by gasoline shortages.

Economic difficulties continued in Michigan into the 1980s, but the 1990s showed more promise. Difficult times returned with a national economic slump early in the first decade of the twenty-first century. Another, more serious downturn began toward the end of the decade, when a financial crisis swept around the world. Michigan, with its big automotive industry, was especially hard hit. In 2009, Chrysler and General Motors even filed for reorganization under **bankruptcy** law. In that same year, Michigan's average unemployment rate reached 15.2 percent, at that time the highest level of any state in the country.

Still, the state has strong economic potential. By 2010, there were signs that auto companies were starting to do better financially. Besides auto firms, many large companies have their headquarters in Michigan. For example, the Dow Chemical Company, one of the largest chemical companies in the world, is based in Midland. These companies continue to provide many jobs for Michiganders. By September 2015, the unemployment rate had fallen to 5 percent and Michigan became the national leader in economic growth.

10 KEY DATES IN STATE HISTORY

1. 300 BCE

The Hopewell people hunt and farm in the area.

2. 1618

French explorer Étienne Brûlé lands at the future site of Sault Sainte Marie, becoming the first European to set foot in what is now Michigan.

3. 1668

French missionary Jacques Marquette establishes the area's first European outpost, at Sault Sainte Marie. The area was already the site of a large Ojibwe village.

4. July 24, 1701

Detroit is founded by Antoine Laumet de la Mothe, sieur de Cadillac. There were one hundred French soldiers and one hundred Algonquin warriors with him. It was named Fort Pontchartrain du Détroit.

5. January 26, 1837

President Andrew Jackson signs the bill making Michigan the nation's twenty-sixth state. A free state, Michigan closely followed Arkansas, a slave state, into the Union.

6. September 27, 1908

The first Model T built at Henry Ford's plant rolls off the assembly line. Ford added a moving assembly line on December 1, 1913.

7. August 26, 1935

The United Auto Workers Union (UAW) is formed as two hundred delegates gather in Detroit. General Motors signs the first contract with the UAW on February 11, 1937.

8. August 9, 1974

Gerald Ford, a former Michigan congressman, becomes president.

9. July 18, 2013

Detroit becomes the largest municipality in the United States to file for bankruptcy, with $18.5 billion in debts. The city emerged from bankruptcy in December 2014.

10. April 25, 2014

Flint switches its water supply to the Flint River. Elevated levels of lead, due to a lack of proper water treatment, are found in the drinking water, and a state of emergency is declared on October 1, 2015.

Dutch heritage is celebrated at the Tulip Time Festival in Holland, Michigan. People from many countries continue to immigrage to Michigan and become US citizens.

The People

Every ten years, the US Census Bureau counts the number of people in the United States. According to the 2010 census, 9,883,640 people were living in Michigan as of April 1 of that year. Michigan ranked eighth in the United States for highest population. Many people in Michigan live in cities, and almost half of the residents of Michigan live in the Detroit and Ann Arbor areas.

Where did all these people come from? According to a 2013 estimate by the Census Bureau, 616,786 Michiganders were born in a foreign country. That is only 6.2 percent of the population, but it is a growing part of the population. The percentage of the population in the state that was foreign born was 3.8 in 1990 and 5.3 in 2000. More than half of the **immigrants** in Michigan have become US citizens, meaning they are eligible to vote.

Trail Blazers

Native Americans in what is now Michigan set up a trail system that would make it easier to trade with tribes in nearby states. Those trails are still in use. The Great Sauk Trail has become US Highway 12, and Interstate 94 follows along the path of the St. Joseph Trail.

Greektown is one of the many ethnic neighborhoods that give variety to life in Detroit.

The remaining Michiganders include people born elsewhere in the United States and people born in Michigan whose parents, grandparents, or other ancestors arrived in the region in the past. Many Michiganders can trace their roots to Britain or France. Others trace their heritage to such countries as Germany, Poland, and Ireland.

Some cities in Michigan have a higher concentration of people from a certain part of the world. For instance, Dutch immigrants settled Holland, Michigan, in 1847. Every May, the people of Holland, Michigan, celebrate their Dutch heritage with Holland's Tulip Time Festival. Some neighborhoods in large cities, such as Greektown in Detroit, are made up largely of people of a certain ethnicity, with traditional ethnic grocery stores, bakeries, and festivals.

Michigan's large population is diverse. The largest minority group in Michigan is made up of African Americans, who represent about 14 percent of the population. Asian Americans make up slightly more than 2 percent. Nearly 80 percent of the population is white. Almost fifty-five thousand Native Americans live in Michigan. People of Hispanic descent (who may be of any race) make up slightly more than 4 percent of the population.

The name "Michigan" comes from a French version of the Ojibwe word *michi-gama*, which means "big lake." The French used the word to refer to the lake now known as Lake Michigan. The name was first officially applied to a land area in 1805, when Congress established the Territory of Michigan.

The French, as the first Europeans to set foot in the region, were very influential in the mapping and the naming of places in what is now Michigan and beyond. Much of this is due to Father Jacques Marquette, who was skilled at learning languages. He was able to carry on conversations in six Native American dialects, especially Huron. It was from Michigan that he departed with Louis Jolliet on his famous exploration of the Mississippi River.

In notes on his travels, Marquette wrote: "On the 17th day of May 1673, we started from the mission of St. Ignace at Michilimackinac … The joy that we felt at being selected for this expedition animated our courage … We obtained all the information that we could from the [Natives] who had frequented those regions; and we even traced out from their reports a map of that new country."

Detroit is Michigan's largest city. Located in the east, on the shore of the Detroit River, the city has played a key role in the state's history—in part because of its location near Canada and along the river that links Lake Saint Clair with Lake Erie.

Moving north or west from Detroit, other Michigan cities include Saginaw, Flint, Ann Arbor, and Jackson. Central portions of the state are home to cities such as Mount Pleasant and Lansing, Michigan's capital. West of Lansing are the large cities of Battle Creek, Grand Rapids, and Kalamazoo. The city with the biggest population on the Lower Peninsula's western coast is Muskegon.

The names of some of Michigan's cities honor famous people. Cadillac was named after the French officer Antoine Laumet de la Mothe, sieur de Cadillac. Marquette was named for Father Marquette. Pontiac carries the name of the Native American leader Pontiac.

People who live in or come from Michigan may refer to themselves by different names. Some say "Michiganders," and some say "Michiganians." There are also people who say "Michiganites." Some residents of the Upper Peninsula, or the UP, refer to themselves as "Yoopers."

The city of Detroit is Michigan's population center. Almost 45 percent of the state's residents live in the Detroit area.

1. William E. Boeing

William E. Boeing was born in Detroit in 1881. He founded the Boeing Airplane Company, which made small planes. Today, Boeing is one of the world's largest aerospace companies.

2. Francis Ford Coppola

Francis Ford Coppola was born in Detroit in 1939. He overcame **polio** as a child to become an Academy Award–winning screenwriter and filmmaker. Among his Oscar-winners were *Patton,* the Godfather series, and *Apocalypse Now*.

Francis Ford Coppola

3. Henry Ford

Henry Ford was born in Wayne County during the Civil War and changed the fortunes of Michigan by developing the assembly line. This revolutionary method of making cars helped Ford Motor Company sell millions of automobiles. He and his family established the Ford Foundation, which funds research, education, and development.

4. Magic Johnson

Earvin "Magic" Johnson of Lansing led Michigan State to an NCAA basketball title, then guided the Lakers to five National Basketball Association titles. Then he established a business empire, bought the Los Angeles Dodgers, and raised HIV awareness.

Magic Johnson

5. Charles Lindbergh

The first person to make a nonstop solo flight across the Atlantic Ocean, Charles Lindbergh was born in Detroit in 1902. In 1927, Lindbergh flew 3,600 miles (5,800 km) in 33.5 hours from New York to Paris. He received the Congressional Medal of Honor.

Charles Lindbergh

MICHIGAN ★ ★ ★ ★

6. Madonna

Madonna was born Madonna Louise Veronica Ciccone in Bay City, Michigan, in 1958. Madonna ranks as the top-selling female recording artist ever, according to the *Guinness World Records*. In 2008, she was inducted into the Rock and Roll Hall of Fame.

7. Larry Page

Larry Page was born in Lansing, Michigan, in 1973, the son of a computer science professor and a computer programming teacher. He went to Stanford University in California for graduate school. He and fellow student Sergey Brin founded Google Inc. in 1998.

8. Jordyn Wieber

This gymnast from DeWitt starred at the 2012 Summer Olympics in London as she contributed to the first US women's team gold medal in sixteen years. She also won the all-around gold medal at the 2011 World Championships in Tokyo.

9. Serena Williams

Serena Williams was born in Saginaw. As of 2016, she has won numerous Olympic tennis medals as well as more than thirty Grand Slam singles and doubles titles. She has earned more prize money than any woman tennis player ever.

10. Stevie Wonder

Stevie Wonder was born Steveland Judkins in Saginaw, in 1950. He became blind shortly after birth. When Motown Records signed him to a contract, the company called him "Little Stevie Wonder." Wonder has won more than twenty Grammy Awards.

Madonna

Jordyn Wieber

Serena Williams

Who Michiganders Are

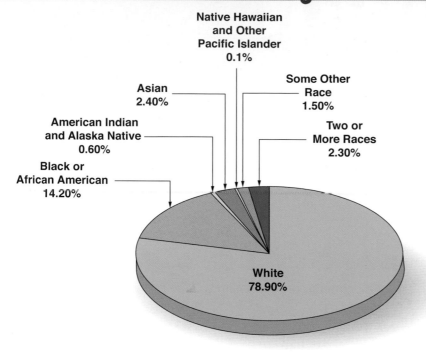

Native Hawaiian and Other Pacific Islander
0.1%

Asian
2.40%

Some Other Race
1.50%

American Indian and Alaska Native
0.60%

Two or More Races
2.30%

Black or African American
14.20%

White
78.90%

Total Population
9,883,640

Hispanic or Latino (of any race):
• 436,358 people (4.4%)

Note: The pie chart shows the racial breakdown of the state's population based on the categories used by the US Bureau of the Census. The Census Bureau reports information for Hispanics or Latinos separately, since they may be of any race. Percentages in the pie chart may not add to 100 because of rounding.

Source: US Bureau of the Census, 2010 Census

Arab Americans in Michigan

Michigan is home to the second-highest number of Arab Americans of any state in the country, after California. A 2013 estimate by the Census Bureau put the number of Arab Americans in Michigan at more than 178,000 or 1.8 percent of the overall population. Wayne County, Oakland County, and Macomb County—all in the greater Detroit area—have the highest number of Arab Americans in Michigan. Arab Americans account for 46.5 percent of the nearly 100,000 residents of Dearborn, in Wayne County. Many of the Arab Americans in Michigan are immigrants from Middle Eastern countries. Others belong to families who have lived in the state for many years.

Like other state residents, Arab Americans in Michigan play an active role in the economy, the government, and other areas of daily life. For example, the Arab American Women's Business Council is an organization in Dearborn that helps women of Arab descent

Famous Visitor

Petoskey has long been a summer destination for people from Michigan and other states. One of the most famous visitors was the writer Ernest Hemingway, who came with his family from Illinois to Walloon Lake for his first twenty-two summers.

Arab Americans are an important part of the Michigan population. Nearly half of the residents of Dearborn are from families that came from the Middle East.

develop their business or professional careers. Organizations such as the American-Arab Anti-Discrimination Committee, a national group that has an office in Dearborn, combats discrimination and hate crimes against Arab Americans.

Diversity

Before the Civil War, many African Americans came to Michigan on the Underground Railroad to escape slavery. During World War II, African Americans were recruited from the South to work in Michigan's automobile plants. Today, nearly 1,400,000 African Americans live in Michigan. Of these, almost half—roughly 650,000—live in Detroit. African Americans in Michigan work in every field, including politics, industry, farming, medicine, and education. In 2001, the first Black **Chamber of Commerce** in Michigan opened its doors in Detroit, with a goal to provide support to African-American businesspeople.

Throughout most of Michigan's history, African Americans in the state had very difficult lives. Even though the state, beginning in 1885, adopted several laws banning racial discrimination, African Americans still did not have the same rights and privileges as white people. African-American children often went to separate schools from white children. Michigan felt the tension as the civil rights movement swept across the United States in the 1950s and 1960s. The civil rights movement fought for equal rights for everybody, regardless of race. As the entire country was struggling with the issue of race, many people worked together to find ways to bring about change. But some people opposed change, and some were angry that change was not occurring faster. There were race riots in several United States cities, including Detroit.

Hispanic Americans and Asian Americans are fast-growing minority groups. More than 4 percent of Michigan's population is made up of people of Hispanic descent. The Michigan Commission on Spanish-Speaking Affairs was created in 1995 to encourage education about and celebration of Hispanic culture and language, as well as to provide services to the Spanish-speaking community. Each year from September 15 to October 15, Michiganders celebrate Hispanic Heritage Month. Festivities include music, art displays, literary readings, food, and dancing. The Detroit Institute of Art features work by some Hispanic and Spanish painters, including Picasso and Joan Miró.

People of Asian Indian ancestry make up the largest group of Asian Americans in Michigan. They accounted for one third of the state's Asian Americans, according to the 2010 census. Chinese Americans made up the second-largest group, accounting for nearly 19 percent of Asian Americans. Korean Americans were the third-largest group, at about 10 percent. Michigan is home to more than twenty-one thousand businesses that are owned by Asian Americans.

Native Americans

Native Americans used to make up the entire population of the region. With the arrival of Europeans and then American settlers, however, their numbers decreased. Today, they represent one of the smallest minority groups in the state.

Some of Michigan's Native Americans live in towns and cities alongside other Michiganders. They work in the same industries, hold government offices, and attend the local schools. Other Native American Michiganders live on reservations spread across the state. These reservations include Bay Mills (Ojibwe), Grand Traverse (Ottawa and Ojibwe), Hannahville (Potawatomi), Huron Potawatomi, Isabella (Ojibwe), Lac Vieux Desert (Ojibwe), L'Anse (Ojibwe), Pokagon (Potawatomi), and Sault Sainte Marie (Ojibwe). Many Native Americans in the state embrace modern life but also continue to practice the traditions of their ancestors. These traditions are also shared with others through museums, presentations, and powwows and other festivals.

City Life

In the early 1900s, immigrants from all over the world came to Michigan. The state's mills and factories brought the promise of work. Struggling families from other areas of the United States came to Michigan during this time as well, hoping for high-paying jobs.

Native American traditions are shared in powwows.

As manufacturing industries became increasingly important in Michigan's economy, the population in Michigan shifted from farms to cities. In 1850, almost all Michiganders lived in rural areas. But the population of towns and cities was rising, and it continued to rise in the following decades. Then, when the United States entered World War I in 1917, the demands on Michigan's automobile industry grew immensely. The military needed armored vehicles, trucks, and other materials. People moved from the farms of Michigan and from elsewhere in the country to work in the city factories to help meet this demand.

World War I ended in 1918. A little more than a decade later, the Great Depression had a major impact on Michiganders. Because few Americans could afford to buy cars, many automobile workers lost their jobs. By 1933, Michigan's unemployment level reached 46 percent, while the national rate stood at 24 percent. Because of the high cost of farming materials—at a time when farmers were getting very low prices for what they produced—many Michiganders stayed in the cities. Others who had been living on farms joined them.

This move to the city has lasted. Today, four-fifths of all Michiganders live in a city or town. The city of Detroit has more people than any other city in Michigan. Even though the city's population has been declining, it had 713,777 residents in 2010, making it the nineteenth most populated city in the United States. About 4.3 million people lived in the Detroit metropolitan area, which ranked twelfth in the US.

Looking to the Future

The population of Michigan grew by almost 7 percent between 1990 and 2000. The following decade saw growth only in some years because the state's economy faced challenges and good jobs were harder to find. Overall, the population of Michigan declined slightly (by less than 1 percent) between 2000 and 2010. But as it has throughout its history, Michigan continues to delight old and new residents alike. The diverse face of cities like Detroit, the beauty of the state's landscapes, and the variety of ways for people to work, play, and enjoy their lives all make Michigan an exciting and enriching place to live.

ArtPrize

Mackinac Island Lilac Festival

1. ArtPrize

Artists from around the world gather in 3 square miles (8 sq km) in downtown Grand Rapids for several weeks in the early fall in a competition that awards more than $500,000 in prizes. Artists must be eighteen or older, but anyone can attend this free event.

2. Mackinac Island Lilac Festival

The island provides a perfect climate for growing lilacs, which are celebrated each June. There are horse-drawn parades, concerts, bicycle tours, barbecues, a dog and pony show, and of course the wonderful beauty and aroma of flowers and trees in bloom.

3. Michigan Horse Expo

The MSU Pavilion for Agriculture and Livestock Education hosts a three-day festival in March put on by the Michigan Horse Council. There is a high school rodeo, and horse pros hold clinics, seminars, and educational events.

4. Michigan Renaissance Festival

A 37-acre (15 ha) site in Holly becomes a sixteenth century village over seven weekends starting in late August. There are jousts, entertainers, a castle, craft demonstrations, and a Children's Realm to satisfy younger visitors.

5. National Cherry Festival

In July, the Lake Michigan shoreline in Traverse City is home to the National Cherry Festival. The festivities include pie-eating contests, air shows, music and art events, parades, marching bands, and rides.

MICHIGAN ★ ★ ★ ★

6. Old Town BluesFest

Lansing celebrates blues music each September with the Old Town BluesFest, showcasing exceptional local, regional, and national blues musicians. The two-day festival takes place in the city's Old Town neighborhood.

7. Plymouth Ice Festival

Each January, Plymouth celebrates winter with a three-day festival. The Plymouth Ice Festival is best known as one of the largest ice sculpture events in the country. Carvers from around the world come to make art out of great blocks of ice. The festival also features live music and entertainment, interactive family shows, and food.

8. Tip UP Town USA

A giant ice slide, carnival and pony rides, a petting zoo, snowmobile races, and an ice fishing contest are all part of this festival held in Houghton Lake. Events are spread out over two weekends each January.

9. Tulip Time Festival

Holland, Michigan, holds its Tulip Time Festival in May. In addition to stunning beds of tulips and other flowers, the eight-day festival features parades, special guests, music, art exhibits, and food.

10. Upper Peninsula State Fair

Escanaba hosts the annual Upper Peninsula State Fair in August. Attractions include agricultural exhibits and competitions, carnival rides, concerts, sand sculptures, displays of historic equipment, and auto racing.

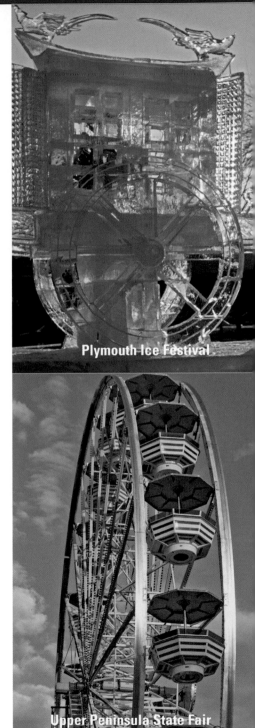

Plymouth Ice Festival

Upper Peninsula State Fair

A statue of Austin Blair, Michigan's governor during the Civil War, stands outside the beautiful state capitol in Lansing.

How the Government Works

Government leaders in Michigan need to balance the interests of big businesses and labor unions, of rural farmers and people who live in cities. Serving the interests of all residents is a large job. Lansing is the capital of Michigan, and this is where Michigan's state government is based. There are also many local governments within Michigan.

Local Government

There are eighty-three counties in Michigan. Each county is governed by a board of commissioners. Members of the board are elected by voters in the county for two-year terms, without any limit on the number of terms. The board of commissioners is responsible for making policies that relate to the entire county.

Each county is divided into townships and cities. Cities have home rule. This means they have more freedom in conducting their business than do townships. There also are villages, which have some of the powers of cities but remain a part of a township. As of 2015,

Silly Law

It is illegal for a person, firm, or corporation to sell, trade, or exchange any car on the first day of the week, which is otherwise known as Sunday.

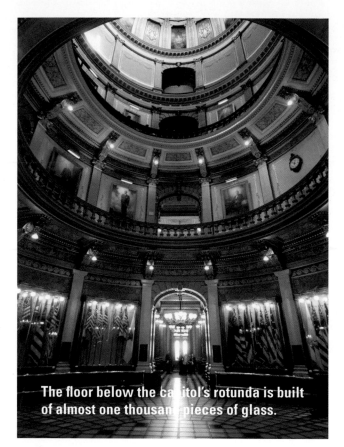
The floor below the capitol's rotunda is built of almost one thousand pieces of glass.

Michigan had 1,123 townships and 117 charter townships. Charters give growing townships extra powers and protect them from being annexed by a city. Michigan also had about 275 cities and nearly 260 villages. Each township, city, and village has its own government. Townships are run by a board of five to seven members. Some cities are governed by an elected council, which appoints a manager to run day-to-day affairs. Other cities are governed by a council and a mayor, who may be directly elected by voters or chosen by the council, generally from among its members. Villages usually are governed by an elected council and a president.

State Government

The Michigan state government has three branches: executive, legislative, and judicial. Each branch has its own powers and responsibilities. The executive branch is headed by the governor. The legislative branch is the lawmaking body. The judicial branch consists of the courts and related agencies.

An elected state board of education oversees Michigan's schools. It appoints a superintendent of public instruction, who heads the state department of education.

The structure and powers of Michigan's government are set by the state constitution. The current constitution was adopted in 1963. It begins with a declaration of the rights belonging to the people. Several portions of the 1963 constitution have been amended, or changed, over the years.

Branches of Government

Executive

Michiganders elect a governor every four years. They also elect a lieutenant governor, secretary of state, and attorney general. A lifetime limit of two terms in office applies to these four positions. The governor is in charge of appointing important state officials, including most department heads, such as the state treasurer. The governor also appoints hundreds of people to boards and committees, signs **bills** into law, and plans the state budget. In addition, he or she can call on the state militia to deal with a state emergency. The lieutenant governor presides over the state senate and acts for the governor in the governor's absence. The secretary of state's duties include management of voter registration, driver licensing, and vehicle registration.

Legislative

The legislative branch of the state government is divided into two parts: the Michigan Senate and the Michigan House of Representatives. Michigan has 38 senators. They are elected to four-year terms. A senator can serve no more than two terms. The state senate is responsible for approving appointments made by the governor. The Michigan House of Representatives is composed of 110 representatives, who are elected to two-year terms. A representative may serve no more than three terms. The legislature is responsible for passing laws, levying taxes, and overseeing the work of the executive branch.

Judicial

Michigan's judicial branch is responsible for interpreting laws and trying cases. The state's highest court is the Michigan Supreme Court, which is made up of seven justices. Ranking below the supreme court is the court of appeals. Michigan is divided into four districts, each of which elects seven appeals judges. The court of appeals and supreme court generally hear appeals of cases that start in a lower court; in an appeal, one side in a case asks a higher court to review the decision that was made in a lower court and determine whether it was fair and in keeping with the law. There are also fifty-seven circuit courts throughout Michigan, and most counties have probate courts that handle wills and guardianships over individuals. More than one hundred district courts handle many types of criminal and other cases. All the judges in Michigan, other than the state supreme court justices and municipal judges, are elected to six-year terms. Supreme court justices are elected to eight-year terms, and municipal judges

In Their Own Words

"As a Michigan senator, I feel a special responsibility to protect the Great Lakes. They are not only a source of clean drinking water for more than thirty million people but are also an integral part of Michigan's heritage and its economy."
—US senator Debbie Stabenow

State representatives work on and debate bills in this chamber in the capitol.

to four-year terms. There is no limit on the number of terms that judges can serve.

Michiganders in Congress

Like all states, Michigan elects two senators to the US Senate. The number of members each state has in the US House of Representatives is related to the state's population and can change after each US census is taken. Based on results of the 2010 census, Michigan has had fourteen representatives since 2013, one fewer than it had for the previous decade.

How a Bill Becomes a Law

When citizens and politicians decide a new law should be made, a bill must be introduced in one of the legislature's chambers. A senator or representative writes the bill, which includes all of the details of the new law being proposed. When a bill is introduced, its title is read. This is the first of three "readings" a bill ordinarily has to go through in each chamber in order to be approved.

Next, the bill is sent to an appropriate committee for discussion. Committees are made up of legislators who have an interest in a certain area. Committees have the power to recommend the bill either in its original form or with amendments. If the bill receives the committee's recommendation, it goes back to the chamber for a second reading. More amendments may be made to the bill at this time. If the bill gains approval to go on to a third reading, the legislators will again vote on the bill. They may decide to make additional amendments. If the bill wins the approval of a majority of the chamber's elected members (for certain types of measures a majority of two-thirds or more is required), it goes to the other chamber of the legislature, and the process is repeated.

Custom Chandeliers

Tiffany's of New York designed the nineteen chandeliers in the capitol in Lansing. The chandeliers are made of copper, iron, and pewter, and weigh between 800 and 900 pounds [363 to 408 kg] each.

If a bill is passed with the same wording in both chambers of the legislature, it is sent to the governor. Sometimes, the second chamber approves a bill only after changing it. If that happens, the bill then goes back to the first chamber. The first chamber may either accept or reject the new wording. If it accepts the bill in its new form, the bill is sent to the governor. If the first chamber does not accept the new wording, the bill is sent to a conference committee. This committee, consisting of a few members from each chamber, tries to come up with compromise wording acceptable to both chambers.

Once the governor receives a final bill, he or she can sign it, and it becomes a new law. The governor also has the power to veto, or reject, a bill. A bill that the governor vetoes can still become a law, but only if the two legislative chambers vote to override (overrule) the veto. For this to happen, two-thirds of the members of each chamber must vote to override.

POLITICAL FIGURES
FROM MICHIGAN

★ Gerald R. Ford Jr.: President of the United States, 1974-1977

Gerry Ford moved from Nebraska to Grand Rapids with his mother as a baby. He attended the University of Michigan. Ford was elected to the US House of Representatives in 1948 and served until replacing the disgraced Spiro Agnew as vice president on December 6, 1973. The following August, he ascended to the presidency when Richard Nixon resigned.

★ Jennifer Granholm: Governor, 2003-2011

The Canadian-born Jennifer Granholm became the first woman elected to be governor of Michigan in 2002. In 1998, she was elected the first female attorney general in the state. She pushed for adding new industries to the state economy and for increasing access to a college education. Michigan was voted one of the best-managed states during her tenure as governor.

★ Mitt Romney: Governor of Massachusetts, 2003-2007

This son of former Michigan governor George Romney was a successful businessman before he was elected governor of Massachusetts. He reduced that state's $3 billion deficit and passed a health care reform program. He lost a race for the Republican nomination for president to John McCain in 2008, but earned the nomination in 2012. He lost that election to Barack Obama.

MICHIGAN

Contacting Lawmakers

To find out how to get in touch with Michigan legislators, go to this website:

www.legislature.mi.gov.

By following the links on the site, you will be able to learn who represents each district in Michigan. Click on "Contact your Representative" to find the names and contact information for members of the house of representatives. Click on "Contact your Senator" to learn the names of members of the senate.

To contact your US senator or congressperson in the US House of Representatives, visit this website:

www.govtrack.us/congress/members/MI.

Road Rage

Budget fights are common in government, but one in Michigan got hotter because residents joined in. Republican governor Rick Snyder wanted to fix damaged roads, but Republicans in the state legislature wanted to cut taxes instead of spending the money to fill potholes.

Groups such as Just Fix the Roads said that bad roads cost residents $357 a year in vehicle repairs and that many people are killed in car crashes caused by roads in need of repair. Just Fix the Roads publishes information about the condition of the state's roads and the way taxes pay to fix them.

In 2015, voters by a large margin rejected a plan to repair the state's roads because they felt the legislature could do a lot better. The bill was confusing as it combined many tax and spending elements. Most voters in the state said they would pay more taxes to fix the roads. By rejecting the legislature's plan, voters sent a message that they wanted the road issue solved on its own.

TechTown at Wayne State University helps new business get started and allows the Baby Boom generation to begin new careers

Making a Living

Michigan is home to many different types of industries, including tourism, manufacturing, and farming. The state has weathered many ups and downs in the economy, but it has always found a way to recover.

Agriculture

Michigan has ideal conditions for agriculture. As of 2014, there were about 51,600 farms in Michigan. The state leads the United States in the production of such crops as blueberries, tart cherries, cucumbers for pickles, and squash. Other crops for which Michigan ranks among the leading states include apples, asparagus, beans, grapes, potatoes, and sugar beets. Corn, soybeans, wheat, sugar beets, and potatoes are the crops that bring in the most money for the state's farmers.

The farms of Michigan are not just for growing crops. Some are livestock farms, where cattle, pigs, sheep, and lambs are raised. Michigan's turkey farms raised more than five million turkeys in 2013. Milk is one of Michigan's biggest farm products. In 2014, Michigan cows produced 865 million pounds (392 million kg) of milk, which ranked sixth in the United States. Dairy brings $14.7 billion into the state each year.

Iron ore mined in Michigan gets loaded onto ships from this dock in Marquette.

Mining

Michigan has a long history of mining, especially in the Upper Peninsula. Some of the minerals found naturally in Michigan include copper, iron, gold, silver, gypsum, slate, salt, coal, and limestone.

Iron ore was mined heavily beginning in the mid-1800s. Iron deposits were found in Marquette, Menominee, and Gogebic Counties in the western half of the Upper Peninsula. But very little high-grade iron ore remains in Michigan. High-grade iron ore has a high proportion of iron. Low-grade iron ore has some iron in it, but it also has high levels of other minerals. A low-grade ore called taconite is still mined in Michigan's Upper Peninsula. Michigan supplied about 23 percent of the iron ore produced in the United States in 2012, second to Minnesota. The two states produce about 99 percent of the iron ore in the US. This iron is mostly used to make steel, which in turn is used for such things as making cars and constructing bridges and buildings.

Copper mining in Michigan began long ago when Native Americans used simple tools to dig for the metal. Between 1847 and 1887, Michigan was the top copper producer in the United States. Copper was mined into the twentieth century. But the state's copper resources were decreasing, and in 1995, the last big copper mine in Michigan closed.

Forestry

Forestry has been an important industry for Michigan. Lumber and wood products contribute billions of dollars to Michigan's economy each year. Unlike minerals that were mined almost until they disappeared, trees are a renewable resource if they are forested responsibly. As trees are cut down for lumber, paper, and other products, new trees can be planted in their place.

The forestry industry went into full swing in the 1840s. White pine—a wood often used to make buildings—was plentiful in the Upper Peninsula. Without trucks to help move wood to other areas, a network of streams, rivers, and canals was used to transport lumber. The huge pieces of wood could be placed on a barge and floated downstream to sawmills and ports. From 1869 to the end of the nineteenth century, Michigan produced more lumber than any other state.

With so much wood available, Michiganders began crafting beautiful furniture. Grand Rapids earned fame as the furniture capital of the world in the late nineteenth century. Today, it still claims the title of office furniture capital of the world.

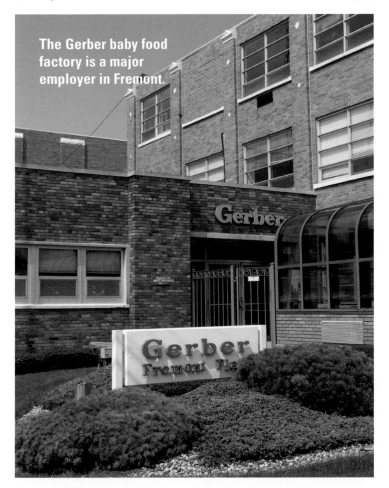

The Gerber baby food factory is a major employer in Fremont.

Manufacturing

Michigan is often associated with the automobile industry. The Detroit area is known as the automotive capital of the United States. Since the early 1900s, Michigan has played an important role in the making of cars. Ford Motor Company, headquartered in Dearborn, was founded in 1903. General Motors began in Flint in 1908 and is now based in Detroit. Chrysler started making cars in Michigan in 1925 and is based in the Detroit suburb of Auburn Hills. Michigan accounts for 22 percent of all the cars made in the United States.

★ 10 KEY★INDUSTRIES

Agriculture

Automobile Manufacturing

1. Advanced Manufacturing

As the automobile industry in Michigan bounced back from the recession, it created more jobs in advanced manufacturing. Detroit and Grand Rapids rank first and third in the US for growth in engineering jobs.

2. Agriculture

Michigan produces more than 70 percent of the tart cherries grown in the United States. Traverse City is called the "Cherry Capital of the World." The state also ranks second in the country in the production of celery, which thrives in the Kalamazoo swamps, and third in the production of asparagus.

3. Automobile Manufacturing

Detroit has long been associated with cars, and despite setbacks, this industry is still important in Michigan. Since 2010, the industry has attracted billions of dollars in investment and created more than thirteen thousand jobs in the state.

4. Christmas Trees

Michigan ranks among the top states producing Christmas trees. The Scotch pine and Douglas fir varieties are among the most popular Christmas trees grown in Michigan. In fact, Christmas trees are among the state's top-twenty most valuable crops. Christmas tree farmers in Michigan harvest more than one million trees each year.

5. Food Processing

Michigan grows a large variety of foods. It is second to California in the diversity of its agriculture as it produces more than three hundred items. These items generate more than $91 billion each year.

MICHIGAN ★ ★ ★ ★

6. Freshwater Technology Services

Farming and advanced manufacturing require clean water. As of 2014, Michigan ranked fourth in the country in blue economy jobs. These jobs work in industries that clean freshwater or are dependent on that water.

7. Information Technology

The state established SmartZones that have encouraged high-tech startups. Centers that help these startups grow from the idea stage to working business include TechTown, which is based at Wayne State University.

8. Iron

Although most of the best iron ore was mined in the 1800s, Michigan is still a major source for iron. Iron from Michigan finds its way into buildings, bridges, and many other structures all across the United States.

9. Supply and Logistics

The bridge between Detroit and Windsor, Ontario, is the largest border crossing in North America, and it links the United States to Canada, our country's largest trading partner. There is a large air hub to Asia, and the state university trains people in logistics.

10. Tourism

With attractions like Mackinac Island, the blues clubs of Detroit, more than 115 lighthouses, and the coasts of four Great Lakes, Michigan is a popular place to visit. More than 150,000 Michiganders work in a tourism-related industry. Travelers spend more than $15 billion in Michigan each year.

Iron

Supply and Logistics

Recipe for Easy Apple Cobbler

Michigan produces delicious apples. Here is an easy way to enjoy them as a dessert.

What You Need

Four Michigan apples

1 tsp (5 milliliters) of ground cinnamon

1 tbsp (15 mL) of butter, melted

¼ cup (60 mL) honey

2 cups (480 mL) granola cereal

What To Do

- With the help of an adult, peel, core, and slice the apples.
- Place the apples in a Crock-Pot or other slow cooker, and mix in the cinnamon and honey.
- Top the mixture with the granola.
- Sprinkle the granola with the melted butter.
- Turn the Crock-Pot on low and cook for seven to nine hours, and turn it on high and cook for two to three hours.
- Top the mixture with milk or yogurt and you have a delicious breakfast or dessert.

Michigan manufactures a lot of other products as well. Kellogg, known for its breakfast cereals, was founded in Battle Creek, where its headquarters is still located. Post, another major breakfast cereal maker, also began in Battle Creek and still has manufacturing facilities there. Gerber, the leading maker of baby food in the United States, sells baby food from Michigan to parents all over the world. Other products made in Michigan include machinery, furniture, appliances, chemicals, and pharmaceuticals. Hundreds of thousands of Michiganders work in manufacturing these and other products.

Tourism and Services

With its many freshwater lakes and rivers, sand dunes, and shorelines, Michigan is a popular place to visit. The tourism industry makes $15 billion per year. It also provides many jobs for the people of Michigan. Some popular places in Michigan to visit include the Henry Ford Museum and Greenfield Village in Dearborn, the capitol in Lansing, the Sleeping Bear Dunes National Lakeshore, the Straits of Mackinac, the Mackinac Bridge, Mackinac Island, the Porcupine Mountains Wilderness State Park, and Tahquamenon Falls.

Summer remains one of the most popular times to visit Michigan. Tourists come to sail the waters of the Great Lakes, enjoy the warm weather, and visit the many natural landmarks Michigan has to offer, such as the sand dunes, beaches, and forests. Spring is a popular time for trout and bass fishing. In the winter months, visitors ski, snowmobile, ice fish, and ice skate. Fall is a beautiful time to drive the hills of Michigan and admire the changing leaves of Michigan's forests.

There are many museums in Michigan. Some explore different aspects of Michigan's rich history. The Public Museum in Grand Rapids is home to a permanent exhibition called Furniture City, which celebrates the state's furniture-making heritage. The Michigan Historical Museum in Lansing brings the history of Michigan alive in its "First People" exhibit. There also are notable art museums, with the Detroit Institute of Arts ranking as the biggest.

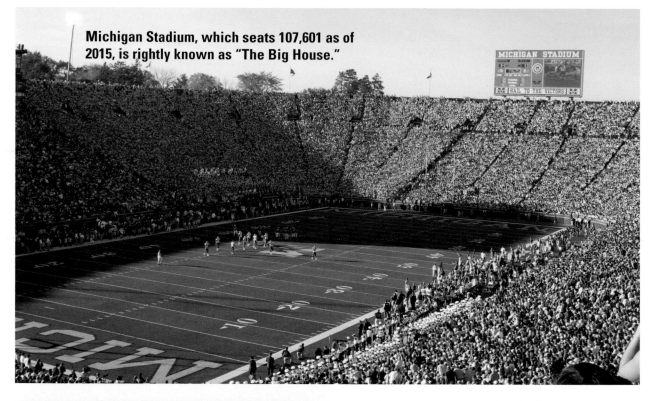

Michigan Stadium, which seats 107,601 as of 2015, is rightly known as "The Big House."

In Their Own Words

"I deeply appreciate the people of Michigan. I love their grit. I love the way they face life. I love the family values they have."
—Former Detroit Tigers broadcaster Ernie Harwell

Sporting events also bring money to the state. Detroit has four major professional sports teams: the Tigers in baseball, the Pistons in basketball, the Lions in football, and the Red Wings in hockey. The University of Michigan and Michigan State University provide top collegiate competition. Residents from around the state and visitors from across the country come to Detroit and to the universities to attend games. The stadium at the University of Michigan, known as "The Big House," was reduced in seating capacity in 2015 to 107,601 but it still holds more people than any stadium in the US. The money spent on tickets, souvenirs, food, hotel expenses, and other purchases helps the state's and the city's economy.

Many music lovers come to Michigan to see the Motown Historical Museum in Detroit or to hear the Detroit Symphony Orchestra. Thrill-seekers visit Mackinaw City to go parasailing over the waters of Lake Huron. Mackinaw City also offers a chance to work through a life-sized maze of mirrors, as does Frankenmuth's Ultimate Mirror Maze.

Whether tourists seek an outdoor, a cultural, or a learning experience, Michigan is a place to find it all.

The tourism industry is a part of the larger service industry. The service industry includes any jobs that provide a service to others. The people who work in stores, sell souvenirs, and manage hotels and restaurants are all a part of the service industry. Bankers, doctors, nurses, insurance agents, and tour guides are also part of the service industry and play an important part in the state's economy. So do teachers. Besides those who work in schools, a large number have jobs at Michigan's many colleges and universities, which also employ scientists and other people in the service industry. The state's two largest public universities are Michigan State University, at East Lansing, and the University of Michigan, which has its main campus in Ann Arbor and branch campuses at Dearborn and Flint.

Protecting the Environment

The state has always depended on the land and its natural resources. Because of this, protecting the natural environment is important to the state. It is so important, in fact, that the Michigan government has worked to educate people about what they can do to keep Michigan clean. Like a number of other states, Michigan takes part in the federally sponsored Conservation Reserve Enhancement Program, which is designed to encourage farmers to help protect soil and water quality and wildlife habitats. Michigan's efforts in this program have focused on the Lake Macatawa, River Raisin, and Saginaw Bay regions. The Michigan Groundwater Stewardship Program aims to prevent fertilizer from contaminating Michigan's groundwater (naturally occurring underground supplies of freshwater).

Michigan also has an extensive **recycling** plan. But it does even more than recycle newspapers, aluminum cans, and plastics. In 1995, it became the first state to start a recycling program for empty aerosol cans, which has helped the environment. In 1993, Michigan began recycling plastic pesticide containers to help maintain the quality of groundwater.

By paying attention to their environment, Michiganders show how deeply they care about their state. Through conservation efforts, they are trying to make sure that the people of the state will always be able to enjoy the beautiful land that Michigan is today.

MICHIGAN
STATE MAP

CANADA

ISLE ROYALE NATIONAL PARK

LAKE SUPERIOR

Copper Harbor
Fort Wilkins Historical State Park

Houghton

Porcupine Mountains
L'Anse Reservation
Porcupine Mountains Wilderness State Park
L'Anse
Baraga State Park
Huron Mountains
Mt. Arvon

Ironwood
Indianhead Mountain
Ottawa National Forest
Marquette
Marquette Bay
GRAND ISLAND

Pictured Rocks National Lakeshore
Grand Marais
Betsy Lake
Whitefish Point

SUGAR ISLAND
Sault Ste. Marie
Lake George
Sault Ste. Marie Reservation
NEEBISH ISLAND
Harbor Island National Wildlife Refuge

Two Hearted River
Seney National Wildlife Refuge
Lake Gogebic State Park
Marquette Mountain
Menominee Range
Lac Vieux Desert Reservation

Marquette River
Escanaba River
Saugatuck River
Hiawatha National Forest
Indian Lake
Manistique Lake
Manistique River
Hiawatha National Forest
Whitefish Bay
Bay Mills Reservation
Lake Nicolet

Ford River
Cedar River
Iron Mountain

Menominee River

Manistique
Father Marquette National Monument
St. Ignace
Fort Mackinac
BOIS BLANC ISLAND
Potagannissing Bay
DRUMMOND ISLAND

Escanaba
Hannahville Reservation
Little Bay de Noc
Big Bay de Noc

BEAVER ISLAND
Cheboygan
Hammond Bay
Rogers City

LAKE HURON

Menominee

NORTH MANITOU ISLAND
SOUTH MANITOU ISLAND
Grand Traverse Reservation
Petoskey State Park
Petoskey
Burt Lake
Mullett Lake
Black Lake
Grand Lake

Sleeping Bear Dunes National Lakeshore
Lake Leelanau
Grand Traverse Bay
Lake Charlevoix
Burt Lake State Park
Pigeon River
Ocqueoc River
Long Lake
Alpena

Torch Lake
Gaylord
Thunder Bay National Marine Sanctuary & Underwater Preserve

Traverse City
Elk Lake
Kalkaska
Huron National Forest
Fletcher Pond
Wolf River
Hubbard Lake

Crystal Lake
Bear Lake
Manistee River
Higgins Lake State Park
Au Sable River
Cooke Dam Pond

Manistee
Hodenpyl Dam Pond
Manistee National Forest
Cadillac
Houghton Lake
Tittabawassee River
Au Gres River
Tawas City
Port Crescent State Park

Hamlin Lake
Little Manistee River
Big Sable River

Ludington
Silver Lake State Park
Marquette River
Big Rapids
Mount Pleasant
Sanford Lake
Saginaw Bay
Bad Axe

Muskegon River
Isabella Reservation
Midland
Bay City
Port Sanilac

Spring Lake
Flat River
Saginaw
Saginaw River
Cass River
Lakeport State Park

Muskegon
Maple River
Shiawassee National Wildlife Refuge
Shiawassee River
Black River
Port Huron

Grand Rapids
Grand River
Sleepy Hollow State Park
Flint
Warren
Saint Clair River

Holland
Saugatuck Dunes State Park
Thornapple River
Lansing
Pontiac
Livonia
Sterling Heights
Lake Saint Clair
Anchor Bay

Kalamazoo River
Yankee Springs State Park
Battle Creek
Jackson
Ann Arbor
Ypsilanti
Detroit
Dearborn

St. Joseph
Kalamazoo
Portage
Three Rivers
Dowagiac River
Huron Potawatomi Reservation
St. Joseph River
Tecumseh
Monroe

Warren Dunes State Park
Prairie River
Cambridge Junction Historic State Park
Adrian
Raisin River

LAKE ERIE

LAKE MICHIGAN

Legend
- Interstate Highway
- U.S. Highway
- State Highway
- State Capital
- City or Town
- National Forest
- Wildlife Refuge
- State Park
- Highest Point in the State
- Mountains
- Historic Site
- National Monument
- Indian Reservation

miles 0 30

N W E S

MICHIGAN
MAP SKILLS

1. Which state park is in the southwest corner of Michigan?

2. Which mountains in the Upper Peninsula are named for an animal?

3. If you drove to the Upper Peninsula from the Lower Peninsula, which National Monument would be just to the west?

4. How many Native American reservations are in the Lower Peninsula?

5. Which state highway follows the northeast shore of the Lower Peninsula?

6. What name is shared by a river, a national forest, and a city in the Lower Peninsula?

7. The state capital is which direction from Holland?

8. What is the northernmost city in Michigan?

9. Which Interstate Highway runs from the shores of Lake Erie to the shores of Lake Superior?

10. Which bay forms the inside of Michigan's thumb? It shares its name with a city.

Manistee River

10. Saginaw Bay
9. Interstate 75
8. Copper Harbor
7. East
6. Manistee
5. State Highway 23.
4. Three, the Grand Traverse Reservation, the Isabella Reservation, and the Huron Potawatomi Reservation.
3. Father Marquette National Monument
2. Porcupine Mountains
1. Warren Dunes State Park

Warren Dunes State Park

State Flag, Seal, and Song

The Michigan state flag was adopted in 1911. It is a blue flag with the Michigan coat of arms in the middle. Near the top of the state coat of arms is a bald eagle holding arrows and an olive branch, a symbol of peace. The moose and elk are symbols of Michigan, and they are supporting a shield with a man standing on a grassy peninsula. The man's right hand is raised in peace, and his left hand holds a gun, indicating his willingness to defend the state and the nation. There are three Latin sayings on the coat of arms: *E Pluribus Unum*, which means "from many, one," refers to the many states that make up the United States; *Tuebor* means "I will defend"; and *Si Quaeris Peninsulam Amoenam Circumspice*, the state motto, means, "If you seek a pleasant peninsula, look about you."

Michigan's state seal shows the state coat of arms encircled by the words "The Great Seal of the State of Michigan A.D. MDCCCXXXV," which in Roman numerals stands for 1835, the year the seal was adopted.

There is confusion about the official state song of Michigan, and it could be because the titles of two songs about the state are so similar. "Michigan, My Michigan" dates to the Civil War, but it is "My Michigan" that was adopted as the state song by the state legislature in 1937. "My Michigan" was written by Giles Kavanagh and H. O'Reilly Clint. You can read the lyrics at: **www.ereferencedesk.com/resources/state-song/michigan.html**.

Glossary

abolitionist	A person who wants to abolish or get rid of something, especially slavery.
alliance	A partnership or relationship between groups that benefits all groups involved.
assembly line	A series of workers and machines on which a car or other item is put together.
bankruptcy	A condition in which a person or a company does not have enough money to pay their debts.
bill	A proposed law presented to legislators for discussion.
chamber of commerce	An association that promotes businesses in a place.
climate	Weather conditions in a region over a long period.
dune	A mound or ridge of sand or other loose material formed by the wind.
immigrants	People who leave one country to live in another country.
longhouse	A wooden, bark-covered house up to 100 feet (30.5 m) in length in which many Native American families could live.
mass production	Making large numbers of similar products quickly.
outpost	A small military camp far from the main group.
peninsula	Land that sticks out into water and is almost entirely surrounded by water.
polio	A disease that affects the nerves of the spine, making it hard to move some muscles.
recycling	Changing waste into a usable material.
strait	A narrow passage of water that connects two larger bodies of water.
territory	An area of land ruled by a country that does not have the full rights of a state.

More About Michigan

BOOKS

Burcar, Colleen. *It Happened in Michigan: Remarkable Events That Shaped History.* It Happened In Series. Guilford, CT: Globe Pequot Press, 2011.

Domm, Robert W. *Michigan Yesterday & Today.* Minneapolis, MN: Voyageur Press, 2009.

Martone, Laura. *Moon Michigan.* Berkeley, CA: Avalon Travel, 2009.

Sobczak, John. *A Motor City Year.* Detroit, MI: Wayne State University Press, 2009.

Vachon, Paul. *Forgotten Detroit. Images of America.* Charleston, SC: Arcadia, 2009.

WEBSITES

Michigan Photographs

www.h-net.org/~michigan/photos/index.html

Official State of Michigan Website

www.michigan.gov

Pure Michigan: Michigan's Official Travel and Tourism Site

travel.michigan.org

ABOUT THE AUTHORS

Johannah Haney writes books and magazine articles from her home in Boston, MA. Growing up in Ohio, she often visited Michigan.

Richard Hantula is a writer and editor living in New York City, but he was born and brought up in Michigan.

Petra Miller is a writer and public relations professional who has lived her entire life in the Midwest. She vacations in Michigan with her husband, two children, and their dog Beaner.

Index

Page numbers in **boldface** are illustrations. Entries in **boldface** are glossary terms.

abolitionist, 36, **37**

African Americans, 37, 46, 51–52

agriculture, 8, 25, 33, 51, 53, 57, 65, 68

alliance, 25

American Revolution, 31–32

Ann Arbor, 35, 45, 47, 73

Arab Americans, 35, 50–51, **51**

assembly line, 38, 43, 48

automobile manufacturing, 14, 34, 38–39, **38, 40**, 41–43, 48, 51, 53, 67–68

bankruptcy, 42–43

Battle Creek, 37, 47, 71

bill, 43, 59–61, 63

Brûlé, Étienne, 25, 28, 43

Cadillac, Antoine Laumet de la Mothe, sieur de, 28–29, 43, 47

chamber of commerce, 51

Civil War, 36–37, 48, 51, **56,** 73

climate, 16–17, 26, 54

copper, 23–24, **24**, 36, 61, 66

Dearborn, 14, 35, 50–51, **51,** 67, 71, 73

Detroit, 14, 29, 31, 33–39, **40**, 43, 45–48, **46, 47,** 50–53, 67–69, 71–73

dune, 9, 12, **12**, 15, 18, 20, 71

endangered species, 18–19, **19**

Flint, 35, 39, 43, 47, 67, 73

Ford, Gerald, 34, 43, 62

Ford, Henry, 14, 35, 38–39, 41, 43, 48

forests, 4, 8–9, 12, 17–18, 20, 28, 39, 67, 71

French and Indian War, 29, 31

fur trade, **25,** 28–29, 31

glaciers, 5, 7, 9, 23

government
    federal, 12, 32, 36, 41, **41**, 43, 46, 60, 62–63
    local, 57–58
    state, 34, 57–63, 73

Grand Rapids, 24, 34, 47, 54, 62, 67–68, 71

Great Depression, 39, 53

Great Lakes, 7, 12–13, 16, 21, 28, 31, 33, 59, 69, 71
    Erie, 13, 28, **32,** 33, 36, 47
    Huron, 5, 8–9, 13, 28, 31, 72
    Michigan, 5, 9, 12–13, **12**, 15, 46, 54, 68
    Superior, **6,** 8–9, **9,** 13–15

Hispanic Americans, 46, 52

Hopewell people, 23–24, 43

Huron (tribe), 25–26, 46

immigrants, 35, **44,** 45–46, 50, 52

iron, 28, 36–37, 61, 66, **66,** 69

Index

Lansing, 34, 36, 38, 47–49, 55, **56**, 57, 61, 71

longhouse, 25

lumber, 4, 20, 36, 67

Mackinac Island, 15, 31–32, 54, 69, 71

Marquette (city), 8, 47, 66, **66**

Marquette, Jacques, **22**, 28, **29**, 43, 46–47

mass production, 38

Michigan State University, 34, 72–73

mining, 23, **24**, 36, 66–67, **66**, 69

Motown, 34, 49, 72

museums, 14–15, 24, 34–35, 39, 52, 71–72

Native Americans, 8, 21, **24**, 25–28, **26**, **29**, 31, 33, 37, 45–47, 52, **53**, 66

Northwest Ordinance, 32

Norton Mounds, 24

Ojibwe (tribe), 8, 25–26, 28, 43, 46, 52

Ottawa (tribe), 24–26, **25**, 31, 52

outpost, 28, 31, 43

Paleo-Indians, 23

peninsula
Lower, 5, 8–9, 12–13, 15–19, 26, 28, 34, 36, 47

Upper, **6**, 8–9, 13–14, 16–18, 20–21, 26, 28, 36, 47, 55, 66–67

Petoskey stones, 5, 15

Pictured Rocks, **6**, 9, 15

polio, 48

Pontiac's Rebellion, 31

Porcupine Mountains, 8–9, **8**, 71

Potawatomi (tribe), 25–27, **27**, 35, 52

recycling, 73

Rosie the Riveter, 41

Sault Sainte Marie, 8, 28, 43

strait, 9, 28–29, 31–32, 71

Tahquamenon Falls, 13, **13**, 71

territory, 26, 32–33, 46

Toledo War, 17, 36

tourism, 65, 69, 71–73

Truth, Sojourner, 37, **37**

Underground Railroad, 37, 51

United Auto Workers (UAW), 39, 43

University of Michigan, 35, 62, 72–73

War of 1812, 15, 32–33, **32**

Wayne State University, **64**, 69

World War II, 35, 39, **40**, 41, 51